"I could not pu
through. . . .A com
　　Hank Owens—Florida Department of Education

"Every salesperson has walked through the tall grasses. . . . I loved it. . . I thought it was wonderful and full of insights into my life. . . It made me anxious to get from page to page."
　　　　　　　　　　　Richard Pasnik— Salesperson

"So much fiction today is fluff and nonsense, and sex. LitTG is a beautiful story full of subtle and yet intense moments for avid readers of any age. I'm sure it will be popular in my library. I will recommend it to everyone I talk to who is looking for a good story with meaning."
　　　　　　　　　　　　　Marion Wager—Librarian

I'm recommending LitTG to all my readers for Middle School and High School students. . . . It rattles the notion that learning happens only in the classroom with a stack of books. Education becomes a process of life. The theme supplies many different situations ideal for the development of thinking skills and values clarification. It makes a masterful statement for allowing nature to teach the true lessons of life.
　　　　　Virginia Knowles—home educator, publisher

"LitTG is a thought provoking book that will not let you put it down. We read it at different times and once begun we had to finish it. The best book we've read this year.
　　Ed and Elaine Herbert—teacher, corrections officer

"I must have read the book 20 times by now. I keep picking it up and reading a few chapters when I have a few minutes to spare. LitTG is extremely well written. It flowed so smoothly into my soul I felt it was written for me. The lessons of life and growing up are the same for all of us, but sometimes it is easy to misplace the really important things. I recommend it for everyone who has or must grow up.
Lois Sheridan—retired military, school volunteer

"The story grabbed me and carried me along. The people of India pride themselves in being eternal seekers. The Master and the boy are classic Indians."
David Man Singh— Indian national and educator

"LitTG had an innocence about it. It took me back to the memories of my own life and growing up. The journey of the boy into manhood allowed me to revisit my own."
Dave Maynard—Firefighter

"LitTG is a gripping and enticing story that sucked me into its philosophical depth . . . . it transcended entertainment."
Riela Foskett—HS student, aspiring writer

"My thirteen year old son and I read this book together. This book helped us discuss some issues that are usually hard to open up about. I suddenly became aware of the fears and uncertainies my son faces on a daily basis even in his public middle school. I would heartily recommend this book to any father or his son."
Dennis Greenwald, Minister

Dedication

This book is dedicated to Walter and Alma Hahn, my wife Nell, and Jason and Heather

Acknowledgments

The author would like to acknowledge the special help and encouragement provided by (in no special order):

    Cheri and Ken Searle
    Monte and Helen Wood
    Joel Hunter
    Marvin and Martha Flanders
    Ed and Elaine Herbert
    Carl Austin
    John and Jennifer Thompson
    David Hall
    John Michael
    Steve Baumann
    Ralph and Sheila Nenna
    The Heart of Florida Civitan

I was hungry and you fed me, naked and you clothed me, homeless and you took me in. You were the hands and hearts of God to me:

    Walter and Ruth Bowles
    Mary and family
    Earle and Nan Oakley
    Ron and Sue Lawton
    Margaret Patterson Wade

Preface

My mother passed on in 1988 at the age of 87. The manuscript you are about to read was part of my inheritance. The fact that it is only coming to light now can be blamed on both of us. My mother spent a lifetime collecting and saving everything she could lay her hands on. She loved to travel and made it a point to end every trip with several more pieces of luggage than when she began; while I now live two thousand miles away from our homestead in Boston, and the demands of my business made my trips back home irregular.

We, my brothers and sisters, were staggered when we were confronted with the amount of goods included in her will. The will and most of the financial matters were resolved within a few months of Mother's death. Organizing the distribution was made more difficult by the fact that our hermitage contained no less than three full attics and several storage rooms. Many thanks in all these matters must go to my dear sister Ann who still resides in our 5th generation residence on Beacon Street.

Every item, be it furniture or keepsake, had been recorded and categorized. The task consumed nearly the last 12 years of Mother's life, dating to her back injury, which severely limited her ability to travel and collect. Ann would not think of going into Mother's treasures without our company; therefore, each trip back to Boston became a special event for all of us. Our trips turned into a sort of a Christmas, regardless of the time of year.

Together with Ann, we would pull out enough items to ensure a full trip home. Then the boxes, trunks or crates would be moved to a family room, where Mother would visit us once again by the thoughtfulness of her gifts. Pictures were always taken and shared with the sibling families. The amount of interchange and trading that developed from these family treasures knit us together as we had never been before. Often Mother would include notes as to why or how she had decided which of us to bless with a particular treasure.

Fourteen months ago at this writing, I went into one of the attics to retrieve, among other things, item #1247-*Aunt Lillian's Trunk*. Initially, it carried with it no special promise. Aunt Lillian was my mother's oldest sister, being nearly twenty years her elder. She was a mystery to us. Aunt Lillian had married a young Englishman at twenty-two, without my grandfather's approval, and left immediately with him for Hong Kong and later to Sumatra which is today Indonesia. He was employed by Beltman's Ltd. At the time, Beltman's was the third or fourth largest mercantiler in Her Majesty's service.

Within five years Lillian's husband was to fall victim to a malaria epidemic. It caused the death of my thirty-two year old Uncle George Goodman.

Aunt Lillian did not return home to Boston to live, again, much to my grandfather's displeasure. She went on into the service of Beltman's as a scriber. In that capacity she traveled much of the world from South Africa to New Zealand, and, of course, England. Many of the beautiful pieces mother passed on to us were dated and labeled as coming from the good graces of Aunt Lillian "in her world tours."

Item # 1247 did not arouse undue interest, first, since all of Mother's bequeaths were unique, and secondly because it was generally considered, between us, that it simply contained Aunt Lillian's personal effects. They had been shipped back to the family after she was killed in a Japanese bombing attack on the Chinese port of Hong Chow in 1938.

Ann and I found a note in the trunk on top of the contents of item #1247. In it, Mother confessed that she had been so busy she never went through it. She left it to me because she considered me the most history conscious of her children. The trunk was now a sort of a time capsule, held for sixty years and fresh as the day it was closed.

Ann and I found any number of personal items: clothes, toiletries, some jewelry, and fifteen different types of currency and coinage. There were stamps from countries all over Asia and the East Indies; these have only just begun to be appraised for current collector value. Towards the middle of the trunk we found the manuscript you are about to read. It was carefully wrapped in a water resistant waxy paper, which had sealed itself over the years.

Aunt Lillian wrote a short explanation on the top sheet of the manuscript (enclosed).

She was commissioned to go to Sydney, Australia by her employer to transcribe and edit the memoirs of a very important Indian businessman. She enjoyed herself thoroughly and became very attached to the author, an elderly gentleman in his late seventies.

Aunt Lillian made two final drafts of the story. She delivered one to the author and kept the second for herself as a keepsake. Upon reading this lovely little tale, we became interested in its author and publication. Aunt Lillian did not name the gentleman, leaving only a blank line where his name should have gone. We have no idea why. Our search assured us that <u>Lessons in the Tall Grasses</u> or any of several possible similar titles was never published in England, Australia, or India.

We considered that the story deserved to be told in tribute to another time and era where fathers and sons still had to struggle to come together and one good teacher could influence a lifetime.

(Enclosure)

On May sixth, 1919, I was summoned to Sydney Australia by my employer to record, draft, edit, and transcribe a copy of the memoirs of _____.

He was a delightful Indian businessman with a shining radiant smile. Even though he was nearly eighty, keeping up with him was a struggle for me at times.

Beltman's Ltd. paid me well for my time and I received a very generous gratuity from _____ when I delivered the final draft to him.

I expect it will be published shortly in India or Australia under the title of <u>Lessons in the Tall Grasses</u>.

I saved the second draft of the manuscript as a memento of this most pleasurable assignment.

      Lillian Goodman April 17, 1920

CHAPTER 1

The place of my birth and my fathers' births for 1000 years has been Kenshi on the banks of the great Ganges River. It sits on the junction of the Rahadi and the Ganges Rivers. Kenshi has been a trading village for millennia. Goods flowed from the Himalayas, down the Rahadi to Kenshi and from there to Calcutta on the Indian Ocean. We, my family, have been merchants for as long as the story of our family has been told. The miracle of wealth was given to my father, for it was in his youth that the railroad came to join the mighty rivers in our village. Kenshi grew almost overnight into a major center of business and trade, and my father, being a shrewd and sound businessman used every opportunity to grow prosperous and respected in that flow of commerce.

My story begins as I approached my 13th birthday. I was a simple naive boy, who took only passing notice of the prominence my father enjoyed when I accompanied him about town. He was very busy and routinely traveled the length of the Ganges all the way to the mouth of the Indian Ocean. He seemed to travel more after my mother died, just before my tenth birthday.

One evening, my father came to me and informed

me that he had enrolled me in a private secondary school in Calcutta. He said that in two weeks I would board a steamship bound down river to continue my education. Father always carried himself in a managerial manner, so I was not accustomed to discussing things with him. Kenshi was the biggest city I had ever seen. I could not imagine what a wonderful place like Calcutta could be like.

Father told me that I had been withdrawn from the local private school for the children from prosperous families. He said that I was to go to the old village master in the morning. Father said that he was leaving to go upriver in the morning, and would not return until three days before my departure. I was to spend my days with the old man and listen very carefully to all he said. I had heard my father mention his name from time to time, but I had never met him. It was a mystery to me why he would send me to the old man, especially now. He lived in the old town and spoke only to the children sent to him by those who could not pay in ways other than barter. I had just become exposed to the wonders of Geometry and Pi and wondered what the old man could possibly do to prepare me for Calcutta.

Nevertheless, at my father's bidding, I marched to the old man's house in the morning. I was dressed in my school uniform and carried the books and pads from my instructors. My trek to his home caused me uneasiness. I was not allowed to venture into that part of town without, my father. I had only been there a few times. I was not prepared for what awaited me. He lived in a hovel, not a house. The old man was frail to the point of concern.

As I look back, my concern lasted only for a moment. It was as if I was enchanted or hypnotized from the moment the old man spoke. His eyes were dark and clear as crystal. They were the eyes of a young man peeking out through an aged and shrunken shell. They commanded attention. His voice was high, almost shrill. It bubbled, and raced, and paused as he spoke his greeting. It was not the voice of an old man, but a brook of water, ever on the move.

Bowing, I introduced myself as formally and respectfully as possible. The old man would have none of it. He gleamed as he grabbed my shoulders and turned me side to side inspecting my profile, while his fingers examined my flaccid arm for muscle.

"So you are Mutatu, son of the rich and important merchant Mutatu, what a fine boy you are. Did your father tell you that I was his teacher at your age? What a shock it was to hear him again, after all these years. I only hear stories of his greatness and business sense."

Proudly, I answered him that my father was known and respected all along the Ganges. I told him that business demanded that Father travel for many weeks at a time. One of the lessons I learned from my father was, "always attempt to avoid giving offense." I assured the old man that my father spoke of him often, with great regard. I was sure it was only the volume of his business that kept him from visiting the old man.

It was a small lie. My father did mention the teacher from time to time in conversations I overheard. He did convey an element of respect, but there was always another element. It was as if the old man had wasted something, or become unfruitful. I did not mention any of this to him, of course, still, it caused me to wonder what purpose my father had in arranging these two weeks.

"And, what is he sending you to Calcutta to learn?" he asked.

"Trigonometry and economics," was my unhesitating reply.

"And, why are you coming to me?"

I was silent. I had no reply. I could not tell him of my uncertainties for fear of offending him and dishonoring my father. I only shook my head.

"Did your father give you any idea what I was supposed to teach you in these few short days before you leave?"

"No Master, only that I was to spend each day with you until he returns from his trip. I think that will be three days before I board the riverboat for Calcutta. He did say that you were going to teach me, but he did not say what."

"Isn't it strange to you that I would meet you only days before you leave? What could his purpose be?" The old man asked the question, but I knew by the twinkle in his eye that he knew the answer. I was tempted to say trigonometry, but it didn't seem possible. Besides, that would have been my wish, not my father's. To me, trigonometry seemed to be like a promised land, not yet visited. Anyway, I kept my silence.

"Well perhaps we can find out together. First, come in. Put your supplies down. You must explain to me what these studies are. This trigonometry, this economics, what are these things? You must tell me of these things. How will they aid you in your manhood?"

I was glad I had not ventured my first guess. I was eager to show the Master my proficiency as a student, but I had to allow that I was not at all sure exactly what trigonometry was, nor was I at all enlightened as to exactly how I would use it. Economics was another matter. I launched into a serious dissertation on the value of economics in the world of business. How you used it to determine prices, measure demand, establish markup. The study of economics was vital to a successful businessman in this mid nineteenth century. The old man seemed incredulous throughout. He responded like a child watching a magician. Each time I made a statement, he would react as if newly enlightened by the power of my presentation.

He asked question after question. If you lost a great deal on one particular purchase, was it acceptable to raise your prices higher to cover your loss more quickly? If people were in great need, was it acceptable to raise your price very high? If you knew a man to be a liar, should you still market your products through him?

He had an earnestness to him. He struggled to understand and twisted his face as he attempted to integrate my lecture into his limited understanding.

I felt proud and knowing as I lectured. I took time to stop and explain my points patiently. At times he would giggle and laugh at his limitations. I began to consider that my father's real purpose could have been to help the old man in his ignorance, and in that, I might see my future more clearly as an educated man. I would have to deal with ignorant, uneducated people, who would need the benefit of my patient wisdom. What a wonderful calling. I could clearly see the need to be dedicated to my studies at the Calcutta Institute. Many would depend upon me.

The old man grew weary of the house and suggested we continue our discussion as we walked. I paid no attention to the poverty of his neighborhood as I explained the importance of truthfulness. He seemed to consider my thinking to be contrary to the day to day practices of life; this led him to ask questions about the application of my precepts. I had to be attentive as I carefully explained the subtle differences.

Was it preferable in business to deal with a skilled

negotiator who could squeeze a profit out of anything, or find a simple honest man who took his profits where they came and did the same with his losses? I had to answer the questions carefully as I did not want to mislead the old man into partial truths. I had to explain the difference between short term gain and long term security to him several times. I heard it from my father, many times, and I was very confident of the clarity of my message. The simple honest man was by far the more attractive choice, for a profit is of little value if you lose future business. Security is based and constructed upon honest people trusting each other and forming relationships that last throughout the years. I must admit that at times I was surprised that the old man had difficulty understanding some of these simple truths. I really expected more from a man of his age.

His simplicity seemed to compel him to turn a truth slightly. When he did that, it brought the topic into an altogether different light. This would demand another careful explanation on my part. I began to be truly surprised at how very much I knew.

CHAPTER 2

I paid no mind to our path. We proceeded out of town along the main river for a kilometer or two. Once we reached the high-water mark, we swung north and east along the old Flood Road. It was used before the dikes and railroad allowed Kenshi to be established permanently. The Flood Road had been abandoned for years. My father would never have allowed me to use it, but that restriction was not needed. I was a city boy. I would never go down the Flood Road alone or otherwise. It led through the tall grasses of the flood plain to the edge of the great forest. It was the kingdom of the tiger and the cobra, not of men.

I did not notice anything about our path, so earnest was my desire to educate the old man. We talked, and we talked. He asked and I answered. He questioned, and I patiently divided the issues for him, so that he could understand.

I was only vaguely aware when we reached the tributary river, and turned again toward home. When we arrived at his hut the old man stopped, his eyes twinkled through the mask of an old man. He thanked me. Would I return in the morning?

It was as though I was released from a trance. The sun hung low in the western sky and shadows stretched away from the bushes and huts. My stomach burned for food. The whole day was gone! It had evaporated into the old man! If I woke up at that moment, I would not have been surprised. It could have been a dream. So many things were so different.

The old man gave me leave by suggesting that perhaps I could explain some of the new wonders of science to him. He had heard about many things, but he had no one to explain them to him. Perhaps, I would do that for him. I promised I would return in the morning, and raced home against the sun that also raced the pursuing shadows to the cover of the western horizon.

When I arrived home, the servants were not as concerned as I thought they would be. Had my father been home, they would have been out looking for me. They knew I was with the old man, and spoke as though they expected my late return. Soon, I was bathed and fed.

I spent the remainder of the evening in the library reviewing information I thought the old man would find interesting. It was then that the emptiness and sorrow for the loss of my mother paid its usual visit. She and I always talked in the evening. I longed so much to be able to tell her of the day with the old man, just like we always reviewed my school days. We were company for each other. Father was usually up and down the river pursuing trade. After she died, his trips grew longer and his stays at home shorter. Since she died, I dreaded the end of each day. I tried to make myself as busy as possible in the evenings. It did not seem to matter, there would always be that moment when a part of me would pull back and look for her.

Lessons in the Tall Grasses

The 'new day' songs of the birds carried me out of bed and to the old man's hut. I was oblivious to all but the thought of a day full of sharing and expounding upon the wonders of the steam engine. I carried my pride and joy, a microscope, brought all the way from Delhi by my father the year before. My teacher at the private school had never used one before. He fawned over it for weeks. I was not sure whether it was me, or the microscope he would miss most. I was sure the old man would be overjoyed.

I also carried a loaf of pressed rice and two chickens crated by the servants. I was not sure what my father had worked out for payment. I was not even sure the old man used money, but I knew the chickens and rice were a proper gesture.

He greeted me with a hand on my shoulder and recognized immediately that the rice and chickens were meant for him. I had a strange feeling that I was beginning to take the steps of a man. This was just another step into the adult world.

Our discussion seemed identical to the first day's, except that we had a different subject. Once again, the old man expressed his ignorance of the steam engine. He became very excited when I showed him the diagrams I brought. We went through every part of the cycle, from beginning to end. He questioned everything. What was this? Why was that?

I realized there was something even more different about this old man. Many adults asked me questions, but often I knew they were questions that an adult allows a child to answer. The old man asked me questions in an unashamed desire to know. He did not care who or what taught him, only that his desire be quenched. Hence, his questions bore to the heart of the machine, and to the limits of my understanding.

I made a little bit of a production out of the microscope. I opened its carrying case toward him, like a magician. He laughed uproariously at the thought of this strange object allowing him to count the hairs on the leg of a fly. He said he had heard of such things, but did not ever think he would live to see one.

I chose that moment to attempt to move into an area of discussion of which I had some questions. "Even the gods would love to look through one of these." I said. I discerned that the old man's expression slipped ever so slightly from gaiety to thoughtfulness. His smile continued, but his eyes studied another question my eyes could not see. "I am getting too old." he said, getting up. "Let us walk."

We took the chickens and rice to the shack next door. I did not stand close enough to listen to the conversation he had with the woman who lived there. I knew I was a little upset at the thought of the old man giving my payment away. That passed when the old man returned to me and thanked me again for my generosity. He said the woman would cook a chicken for the evening meal. I could eat with them if I wished.

Our path took us out of town and down the flood road, again. I brought some slides with me to collect specimens for the microscope, but after what had happened I was not sure he wanted to look into it any more. When I showed him the slides and my specimen kit, the spirit of the previous day's walk returned. As we walked, I showed him each piece and explained its purpose.

We collected several promising specimens. This day our conversation did not stop me from noticing our surroundings. I was confronted by a desolate forbidding aisle of arched grasses and bush rising up two meters and more over our heads. I was concerned. This was a dangerous road. I was so taken up with my lecturing the day before, I scarcely noticed our surroundings.

The concern lasted only until the next question took me, again, into the role of enlightened lecturer. I saw, again, the burning desire within the old man to know, to understand all that was possible. I began to realize that wisdom and knowledge were not the same things and this old wise one was compelled by his wisdom to pursue knowledge even if it came from a precocious child, like me. What a wonderful compliment.

CHAPTER 3

Our conversation carried us down the path. At one point, the old man slowed and stopped next to a flowering bush. He motioned me over to him.

"I have something to show you." he said. "I have looked at this over and over again, since I was a young man. I still cannot understand it. Do you see these ants on the bush?"

I squinted to adjust my eyes. Finally, I managed to locate tiny ants marching in orderly rows on the stalk.

"Yes, I see them." I said, trying to pretend interest. "Do they bite? Are they stingers?"

"Just watch for awhile. Try to follow their path. Look how it leads to the base of the leaves. Now, look closely. See the white specks on the leaf stems?"

"The ants are eating them." I replied. "What is so unusual about that?" I could not see any reason for stopping.

"No, you are wrong!" he replied patiently. "They do not eat the specks. I have watched them in the morning as they carry the specks up the stalks. In the evening, I have seen them carry the specks down again, but they do not eat them. It is as if they are using them."

Still unimpressed, I said, "They are only ants, perhaps they do not have a reason for doing what they do. In school, they call such behavior 'instinct.' Animals do things because they have always done them. There does not have to be a reason."

"Perhaps, it is so," the old man mused, "but, I never found it to be so. I have seen so many things that did not seem to make sense, when I first saw them. After I studied and watched for awhile I always found that there was a reason, a purpose behind everything that happens. I have seen it so often, I simply cannot accept that anything can happen without a reason."

He began laughing, "Except for men that is. I see men doing things all the time that do not make sense."

I was just trying to think of some gentle way to get the old man back on the path, when I remembered my specimen kit. "Let's gather some of the specks and ants for my microscope." The old man became excited at this suggestion. I proceeded to get a couple of each.

Just as I closed the kit, the old man shouted. "Look! It's a war! I thought it would happen. It always does if you watch for awhile. See this beetle; he's trying to fight his way down to the specks." His voice had lowered by the time I was close enough to see. He described the action with the trained voice of a scientist.

In disbelief, I watched as a large beetle was swarmed over by wave after wave of the ants. It became obvious to me that a war was, indeed, being fought over the tiny specks. Some sort of alarm had sounded. The ants stopped industriously caring for the specks in their regulated movements and swarmed toward this giant attacker.

"They're eating him." I cried.

"Just watch." the old man said slowly. "See there."

he said pointing. "Some of the ants are moving the specks away from the battle. I watch these battles often. It is always the specks the beetles are after, never the ants."

I watched the battle rage. The beetle fought his way through the lines of defenders. They, in turn, swarmed over him, pinching and clinging to any organ they could grasp. Finally, the beetle reached the first stems which held the specks. It began to devour them as quickly as its front legs could shovel specks to its mouth. All the while frantic ants were saving as many as possible and running in the opposite direction.

"Isn't it awesome?" giggled the old man. "Do you think we could watch this through your microscope?"

As we watched, the old man described the action to me with obvious intimacy. He pointed out the things to look for with an understanding eye. As the battle raged, he showed me the reinforcements teeming up the stem. Activity was everywhere and frantic. Some ants moved the little pods of white specks from nearby leaves. The beetle was engulfed in a raging mass of ants, trying to pierce his armored shell.

Then it was over. The beetle turned in retreat, shedding scores of ants with each movement. He unfolded his wings and flew to a nearby branch. Once there, he worked his arms and legs to shake the last of the ants loose. He began to inspect each part of his anatomy, passing parts through his mouth as though applying ointment to the wounds inflicted by the ants. One ant still held a death-grip on the beetle's rear leg. He rose purposefully to one side and swiped the ant off.

"What do you think he is doing?" asked the old man.

"It appears to me that he is licking his wounds and applying his saliva as a balm to his injuries." I replied.

"That is correct, but, there is more. Look at the tiny,

tiny hairs on his leg. See how he is primping them up so that they stand out after he passes his leg through his mouth? I think he does this to help protect himself from the ants. As soon as he is done, he will attack again."

I could not believe this was possible. "How could the specks be so tasty to him?" I asked. It seemed too much to endure for such a small prize.

"I cannot say for sure, but thanks to your microscope, I think we shall be able to make a good guess."

"That is called a hypothesis by scientists." I informed him. "First, they observe and gather information. Then, they guess as to why things happen the way they do."

"Well," he chuckled, "I guess that makes me a scientist. I have done that all my life, and many people thought I was a little off, if you know what I mean."

I felt a pang of guilt for my father. I realized that was how my father looked at the old man. This revelation made me confused, for I could not understand why my father removed me from the private school with so little time left before the beginning of my real education.

"There he goes." the old man announced. I was dumfounded as the beetle launched himself and flew to another branch where the battle was joined once again.

"Master, tomorrow I will bring along a magnifying glass. I did not think of it today, but it would be perfect for watching the battle. If it is still going on, that is."

"Oh, my boy," he said, "this battle is being fought in bushes up and down the road. At this moment, we would be able to find the same thing happening on the next bush like this one. The same thing happens on all of them. So you see, the plant must have a part in this mystery, too."

As we continued our walk, I began to consider that

something unusual had happened. I really meant it when I called him Master. Until that moment, I used the term 'Master,' but only as a title of respect for his age and because my father sent me to him. The image of this frail old man did not call to mind any image of a master. Now, I found I was being captured by his world. In that world, he was a master.

CHAPTER 4

As we continued on our way, the Master began to tell me of other mysteries. Each filled my mind with anticipation. Suddenly, he grabbed my arm. I was not prepared for the firmness and strength I felt.

"What is it?" I asked. "Why have we stopped?"

The Master pointed to a tuft of grass no more than three steps ahead. My eye saw nothing, until it saw an eye. Then there were two. An evil hood lifted the eyes almost to my waist. A body the thickness of my leg attached the hood to the ground. Adrenaline flushed through my body. Now it was I who held onto the Master's arm to keep from falling over backwards. He stood firm and still without a sound. The only reason I did not run was the resolve I gained from the Master.

"Hello, my sleek and shiny friend." the Master began. "We did not mean to disturb your hunt. We are only passing by. May you eat many rats today."

He moved us back another step as he spoke.

The snake seemed to relax a little at the friendly gesture. He lowered himself slightly, but remained hooded. Swaying back and forth, he measured us with cold fearless eyes. Finally, he lowered himself and began a purposeful course across the opening.

The snake moved deliberately. It was obvious that we were not the object of his attention. He was continuing his hunt. I noticed that each time he swung his head to the side, he brought his gaze back to us. It was as if our apology was accepted, but not trusted fully.

As the snake moved away, the old man began to follow it.

"Master, where are you going?" I yelled in an unbelieving whisper. "We have escaped the fangs of the evil one. Let us not tempt the gods any further."

"So," whispered the old man, "you consider that we are the ones who have escaped. I think it is the snake who is relieved. He thought we were going to eat him. He was simply informing us that he was a formidable foe, one who would not be easily eaten. We only need to be respectful. Let us follow his hunt for a bit. Our presence may bring him a bit of luck."

Exasperated, I asked him, "How could our presence bring him luck?"

"Every creature out here knows that we can be dangerous. We are hunters and killers," he replied. "The snake hunts in silence. His prey almost never knows he is there until it is too late. We may frighten a rodent by our presence, as the rat flees us, he may run to the snake. Thus, we would have aided his hunt."

I was vaguely aware that many times we startled small animals, but it never entered my mind that we could be effecting the life and death of others.

"I'm not sure I want to help a cobra do anything." I replied.

"I'm afraid we, humans, do it anyway," he replied cheerily. "We build our towns and homes so perfectly for the rats to thrive. They are the reason so many people are bitten. The snakes are not trying to kill us, but the rats. This snake was a wild snake anyway. He is different from the city snakes. He doesn't see many people. It is the city snakes that don't like people. They have been bothered and taunted by humans enough to be dangerous during any encounter."

The snake disappeared into the undergrowth as he talked, and we returned to our original course down the road.

For the first time, I was fully aware of where I was. We were walking through a mixture of forest and grasses. Even the grasses were forbidding in their height and density. The encounter with the cobra served to remind me that we were far away from the town. A train whistle blew in the distance. It seemed that my life and safety were represented by the train, and they were in a far distant place.

"Master," I said, "that was a cobra, what if a tiger finds us? Surely, he will not think we are trying to eat him."

"That is a real possibility," the old man mused, "but my experience leads me to consider that animals, all animals, eat what they are used to eating. Perhaps, that is why we eat rice every day. It is the food that humans eat. I suppose there are many other grains and seeds that we could grow and eat, but we eat rice because that is what we eat. When I was younger and went often into the wilds, I got to know some tigers a little bit. Did you know that every tiger has different stripes; or that you can tell them apart by foot prints they leave? It was strange, but I knew some tigers who seemed to eat only wild pigs, and others who would rather eat deer. It seemed that one would hunt for pigs and another for deer, and that was what they would kill. Besides, we don't give tigers a chance to get used to eating people. Whenever a tiger kills a man, we kill every tiger in the area. Do we not?"

"I guess you are right Master, but, since we left the cobra, every shadow is a tiger in waiting for us."

"If we are eaten by a tiger, I promise you that we will not see him before he attacks." said the old man, as if he were trying to comfort me.

"What shall we do then?" A mixture of irritation and fear filled me. Perhaps the people who thought the old man was a little off were right. Perhaps, this would be the day when a lifetime of ignorance and foolishness would be repaid by a hungry tiger. It would be unfortunate if the promising son of a wealthy merchant perished with him.

"Master, this road belongs to the tigers." I said, trying to sound like an adult talking to a child. "We do not belong here."

"Is it the tiger you fear or death?" he asked.

I paused before I could respond. It was such a ridiculous, irrelevant question. What possible need was there to separate the two?

"I suppose it is not the death so much as the picture in my mind of the tiger tearing us apart, and feasting on us after we are dead." I said, trying to make the image as horrible as words could make it.

"It is an awful thought." agreed the old man, but his steps continued to take us deeper into the tall grasses.

"Why do you continue then?" I said, planting my feet firmly. "Surely there is a safer path we can walk."

"I suppose you are right." he replied in a cheerfully agreeable tone, but his feet continued slowly down the road.

"Then, why do you go further!" I was outraged. Perhaps, he had nothing to live for, but I did. "We must turn back, now!" I said firmly, sounding as much like an adult as I could.

He stopped and turned to look at me.

"How can you be sure?" he said. "How do you know the tiger does not wait behind us, and in turning we walk into his jaws? Perhaps, if we continue we will be walking away from death. Who is to say, until that moment when death introduces itself?"

Now, I was perplexed. This senile old man was treating death like an unwanted acquaintance. Of course, he could say that. He was old enough to be ready to die, but my life stretched before me.

"Master, please do not even suggest such a thing."

The old man began to walk again . . . . forward, down the road. I hesitated for a moment, but only for a moment. I ran to catch up and, for a while, we walked silently side by side.

I could tell the old man was waiting for me to say something. I began to be ashamed for my fear. It was as if I had somehow failed a test of manhood.

Finally, the old man said, "What will you do in Calcutta?"

"I already told you." I said, irritated again. "Father is sending me to school there." I knew there was more to the question, but the old man continued on in silence. "Calcutta is a fine and wonderful city, the likes that village people like us seldom see." He did not seem impressed by my arguments, and again we continued in silence.

"Do you think . . ." he said pausing, "that death does not visit Calcutta?"

The thought never occurred to me. Whenever I imagined Calcutta, I thought only of wonderful prosperity and activity. I realized that the old man was trying to tell me something. Something that he knew and I did not. I was again confronted by my foolishness. I was a child and knew nothing. The helplessness that fear births began to crawl over my mind. The future became a bleak unknown.

I walked on in silence feeling little, alone, and very stupid. What did I know of anything? What a foolish child I was. The old man must be laughing inside himself, as he considers my ignorance.

"You are too serious," he said reassuringly. "Do not be too concerned. God willing we will finish our walk, and God willing you will live a long and prosperous life."

CHAPTER 5

"'God willing.' What do you mean Master? Which god?" This time, he brought the subject up. The Master spoke the phrase differently than I was used to hearing it. People usually said, "If the gods are willing." Or else, they would name a particular God, "If Shiva desires it."

"Which of the gods, do you follow? Who is it you call upon?" My question was simple and sincere, but again, I could see that it affected the Master. He studied the ground ahead of him and continued walking.

"I'm afraid I do not know." he said simply without any show of emotion. "I am not adequate to answer these questions, so I do not begin to pursue them with my students."

So, he did consider me a student. It was a sobering moment for me. I began to realize that I had been led by the old man. Nothing we did was by chance. He was the one who knew where we were going.

"Master?" I said.

As I look back now, I see many beginnings in my life. Until that moment, I paid him lip service with my mouth by referring to him as Master, but in my mind he had been a frail old man, and less. That moment marked a point in time for me. My young mind realized that this frail old man was worthy of that title. I would never again refer to the Master any other way.

The moment that old man became my Master something new began for me. Over the years, I found myself in situations where wonderful opportunities became available to me. Often, they were wrapped in human packages that were less than impressive. I remember the Master whenever I am tempted to discount what someone is saying because they do not appear as I think they should.

"Master, why are you not adequate? Why will you not discuss the gods with your students?"

He sighed resolutely. It was as if he knew that this time he introduced the subject and fairness demanded that he attempt to explain himself. The Master, who just became my teacher, began slowly. His high pitched voice was tightened like a string ready to break.

"In my whole life," he began, "I have seen a need to know. I have looked and studied and sought. I have seen things that made me feel special and blessed to be alive. I have seen special things alone in the grasses and surrounded by crowds of people pursuing other things. I have watched spiders of the same type, spin the same web, starting from the same single strand for fifty years. How can that be?"

He paused and looked at me, as if trying to find a way out of a puzzle, at a loss for words.

Haltingly, he said, "I . . have stood alone . . under the night sky . .and . . heard . . the whisper . . of GOD." His voice quivered and his eyes squinted to keep the tears welling there from rushing down his face. Now that it was said, the words came quickly. "It was the whisper of GOD. Not a gaggle. Not a conversation of the many. There was no chaos. No greater and lesser gods striving to see that their particular agendas be met."

He paused again. This time the tears did stream out. His voice was a high helpless whisper. "I have heard the voice of God. One great, awesome one, but I do not know what name to call out.

I have risen with the sun to burn away the morning mists on the river, and I have heard Him. I sit before the full moon and He sits with me. 'It is good.' He says. 'It is ordered. It is consistent, and I have made it just for you to see, so that you could know Me.'

But, . I . do . not . know . His . name!" He struggled to make each word.

I was frozen in myself. I was not ready for what came out of him and unable to speak. The pain I saw in his face was the only thing I knew. It was my pain for my mother. It was my anger and my hurt, except that I knew I would never see my mother again.

The Master gathered himself, "You see why I do not wish to speak of the gods? It makes me so serious. I know only, that I have heard only one god. In all the things I have seen, I have only seen the hand of one god. The whisper and the hand, they are one, but what kind of a god is that? And, what is in between?" He was laughing again.

"I warned you," he said. "There are so many gods with so many names, and the only God I know does not fit any of the names that I know. None of them can capture the substance of the one I have heard and seen. I told you, I did not wish to discuss these things. They are better left to your father."

He sighed deeply.

"What shall you do then?" I asked, for lack of anything else to say.

"Oh." he said. "It is only an inconsequential thing. How lucky can a man be? How blessed is a man who has heard and seen what I have? Is there anything else?

You showed me your steam engine, and I said to myself, 'Yes, that is Him.' I see him there in the purpose and order. All the parts work for a purpose. I see the same in the specks and the ants and the cobra. Even when I cannot see the reason, I see the order. I see order everywhere, but in the heart of man. And who am I to understand these things? What foolishness it is.

I am just a man. I am an old man. Soon, I shall pass through this thing we call life. You are young. Such things concern you lightly."

"I wish it were so," I admitted, "but it is not. Since my mother died, I think often of such things. She used to put me to bed each night and we would talk, then. Father is a business man. He has many things on his mind, too many to be able to listen to what happened during my day. When I found myself alone, all alone, I gained no comfort from any of the offerings or ceremonies for the dead. Yet, when I am alone and cry into the night . ."

It was time for tears to fill my eyes.

"When I call into the night . . . it is as if . . ."

"You are not alone." He finished the sentence for me. As I nodded my head, a rush of emotions and tears gushed out of me. He pulled me to himself and embraced me as I sobbed. I was a little child again. As the frail old man held me in his arms, I felt only the strength of his years. He felt as strong as anyone could be. We stood there in the wilderness. When my tears passed, I looked up to be comforted by his smile. "You are not alone." he whispered.

As the emotion of the moment left me, I was able to continue refreshed as though I had taken some kind of bath for my soul. I never talked to anyone about my mother. This day, the words came easily.

"Yes," I said. "It is as if I am not alone. I am not sure that it is her. I am only sure that I still feel loved and cared for, and I know the love and care I feel. The love I feel is her love."

We were walking, again.

"I spoke wrongly of you. I misjudged you, again." he said. "I apologize. You have been asking the same questions I asked. Perhaps, you will be given an answer."

We walked again in silence for a while.

"Master?"

"Yes."

"You said you had misjudged me, again?"

"I thought you would be like your father."

He chuckled for a moment as he remembered. "He was so pig-headed, so stubborn. If he couldn't see something, count or measure it, he had no use for it. Ideas were useless to him if they did not lead to something you could hold, but he was always a good boy." I think the Master saw that my mouth was open, and realized that I had never heard my father talked about like that.

"He always tried to tell the truth, like you do." he said attempting balance his statement for my benefit.

I felt a pang of guilt. If the Master knew what I thought when I first met him, he might not think so much of me. I considered that I was the teacher. The guilt I felt mixed with foolishness. Did I dare to ask another question?

"Master?"

"Yes."

"What question did I ask? What question did we both ask?"

"I do not know if I should continue this conversation. . . Do you consider yourself religious?" He stopped and looked squarely at me as he waited for my response.

"I am not sure what you mean. The gods are so far above us. Their activities and purposes are so varied. One battles to bring rain, while another strives to keep the land dry. One brings life, another death. Every one of them has their day, their time in power to control. They do not show the mystery of their purposes and plans to me."

The Master put his hand on my shoulder. "I am a man, but an old man, an old man who does not know anything of these things. I think that it would not be right," he paused and looked for the proper words, "for me to talk to you about matters like this." He stopped again and twisted his face in thought. He looked at me deeply. I heard him draw a breath. Then there was silence again, and we walked. For once in my life, I was silent. I waited. I knew if I waited I would hear the burdens of a man who did not share the burdens of most men.

"It is," he said, "an obligation. As a teacher, I must lead you into truth, as much as I am able. I do not think I should take the chance to lead you into untruth."

"Master," I said helplessly, "I am not sure what we should not talk about."

"I do not want to talk to you about a god I cannot name. Your father and the priests can tell you all about all the gods. If I were to talk to you about what I think, . ." he stopped again, "I know nothing. I could not bear it if I led you or any of my students astray."

I walked on silently.

Finally, he said, "I was taught all the same things you have learned. One does this. Another does that.

Endlessly, they struggle and pull against each other. All these things were beyond my understanding.

When I became a man, I found this need within myself. It called to me, saying that nothing was of value if it did not fit with everything else. I studied. I looked. I learned to read. That was a struggle in itself for a man of my birth.

I would work. I would do anything to live, if I saw hope for the next step." His voice became lively as he talked. His gestures were full of the vibrance of a young man as he related the labors of his youth.

"Finally, I stopped and looked around me. Everything I saw seemed to be meaningless chaos, just like the gods. But, as I was still, as I watched, I began to see order in the chaos. Each time I encountered something that seemed to have no purpose, I studied it. I found that nothing is without purpose. I found it so often enough to believe that it is some kind of law.

One evening I was sitting under the moon thinking and it came to me. Each time I saw order and purpose in something, it was always the same order. It was beautiful. It was perfection. I saw perfection."

His voice had become high and strained with emotion.

"And it was all one! It was only One. I heard Him whisper to me that night. 'Desire me. Seek me. I want you to know me. I am here for you.'

I heard it. I heard it. I heard it, as clearly as if you said it." His voice strained even further as it crackled with a mix of emotion. It was, at once, angry and helplessly frustrated.

"It is not right for me to talk this way to you." he said weakly.

"No Master." I replied, "Please. I have many such questionings myself. You told me it is good to question. Whom shall I ask, if not you?"

"Your father, for one," he replied somewhat tersely, "or one of the priests."

"My father will not speak of such things to me. He says to visit one of the temples. When I talk to the priests, they talk and talk. They tell me the names. They speak blessings and curses, but sometimes they say different things. When I point them out, they become indignant and tell me, I am close minded.

Now you say you have heard a god speak to you, but you will not speak to me of it. Where shall I go?"

"You win. You win." he laughed. "We will speak of it. It will be the subject of our discussion tomorrow."

Once again, I woke from a dream. Shadows stretched across the streets. A day had disappeared from my life, again.

"Will you stay for dinner?"

I looked next door and saw the whole family of the woman waiting for the Master. There were four children and two elders besides the woman's husband. I saw one chicken was still crated and wondered how thin the broth would have to be to feed so many. I would have a full table of food waiting for me at home, so I excused myself.

"What of the specks?" the Master wondered. "Shouldn't we look at them?"

"We will have to wait until morning." I said. "We need the light of the sun to see through the microscope. I think the specks will keep."

Again, I raced against the sun to home.

CHAPTER 6

The servants had everything ready for me when I arrived home.

Silke and Faude were married, but never had children. My earliest memories included them. It seemed strange to me that I talked less and less with them, since my mother's death. They always joined in our evening discussions. My mother had been a glue that bonded us all into a family.

This meal was different; however, Silke asked me about our day. I must have used an hour describing the encounter with the cobra and the ants, but I did not mention anything of our discussion of the spiritual. Their faces beamed as they listened to my adventures.

Finally, I asked them, "What do you know of the Master?"

"He is like a holy man." replied Faude. "He is different from all the other teachers and priests. If I had a son, I would give my son to him. Your father is one of many in this city who prosper today because of him."

"My father is a wise astute business man and trader."

I protested. "The Master does not speak or know of such things."

Faude smiled, then he recited a list of names to me. It included almost all of the prominent men in our city, even the governor, who was one quarter English.

"It was the Master who filled this town with wise men." he said. "We could not believe it when your father began your education without including the Master. Your grandfather ended his working days at the Master's house. The Master was much younger than your grandfather, but your grandfather enjoyed talking with him often. Has the Master never said anything of him?"

"No," I replied, "he has never even mentioned Grandfather."

"Well," insisted Faude, "that does not change how it was."

Now it was I, who had a mystery to solve.

Morning brought its own agenda. I raced to the Master's hut. I was as interested in looking at the specks under the microscope as he. He was sitting in the shade next to the hut talking with three other men when I arrived. He motioned me to approach them and rose up to greet me.

"No . . . No," he said wearily back to the men, "I am going to die soon. This one is the last."

He put his arms around my shoulders.

"He is the last, and he may be the best. His heart is right. Men can learn things quickly, but the heart must be right. His heart is right."

The men appeared to accept his statement gracefully. They bowed and left. Two of them were merchants, like my father. Their sons were in the private school I attended. The other was a metal worker. His son worked with him as his apprentice.

"What did you mean? This one's the last." I asked as the men moved away.

"You are my last student." he replied simply. "When they heard I accepted you, they came to me. They all have sons. They wanted me to include their sons, but it is not possible. I think they understand. I explained it to them."

"What is the reason?" I wondered.

"It was a promise."

"To my grandfather?"

"Yes," he said slowly. "Your Grandfather was a special man. I see him in you. He made it possible for me to live as I do."

"What do you mean?" I interrupted. "You live in a . . a . . ." I could not think for a nice word for a shack. "You live here! You live with the poor. There is no goodness or comfort here. If my grandfather made this happen, you should hate him."

"What I have, I have chosen to have." he said. "I am a free man. I do not labor. I do not sweat and strain to live. Your grandfather made all of that possible for me."

"But, you don't have anything," I protested.

"You do not understand," he said. "Your grandfather loved me. We talked, even as you and I talk. He loved the freedom I had. He had his business. His business demanded his time. He could not go where I went. He could not see what I saw, but he loved it and longed for it.

You remember when I told you what my life was like? How I would work anywhere and do anything. When your grandfather found out I could read, he promoted me in his business. Later he paid me to teach your father. There was no school here at all then. We became friends. After he came to know the desire of my heart, he made it all possible for me. So, even though he could not go, he allowed me to go in his place."

"To the Flood Road?" I asked as sarcastically as I could while remaining respectful. "To the tall grasses? To the door of death? What value do these places have in the world today?"

"Is that all you see?" he said, now thoroughly amused. "Death could come in a small cut. You could cough today and be dead in two days? Do we not live each day at death's door? The question to me is not where death's door is, but when it will open."

He was chuckling at this horrid thought when he remembered the specks and the microscope. I was not ready to surrender the issue, but I did not have any choice.

CHAPTER 7

The Master pulled me into the house
"Let's see the specks," he insisted impatiently, "I have been waiting fifty years to solve this mystery. I thought I would die in my ignorance."

It was easy to set up and focus the microscope. I used the lowest setting, and an image came up to me almost immediately. Startled, I stepped back quickly from eyepiece.

"What is it?" he demanded. "What frightened you?"

"It was the black eyes," I said defensively, "but I was not frightened. It was like it was looking at me."

"Eyes," he said joyously. "They have eyes! They are alive." he exalted. "I knew it! I knew it! I knew it!" he sang. As he sang, he danced a little jig and circled around the floor. He moved his body side to side, and held his arms over his head snapping his fingers.

"Look for yourself," I offered, "they even have legs." It did not seem appropriate to me that a man of his age should carry on like that.

When the Master looked into the microscope, he let out a gasp. "Ooohh," he said slowly, "you are so beautiful my little friend. But, why do the ants guard you, and the beetles endure all to eat you? Why are you so special to them?"

He backed away from the microscope and began to

shout. "It's not fair! You are not fair to me!" He was dancing again, but this time there was anger and aggression in his movements. "You have done it to me again." he complained. "Am I a plaything? Do you get pleasure out of making me sizzle like water on a griddle?"

"Master, what is wrong? I thought you would enjoy the revelation."

"So did I," he said helplessly as he lowered himself to a bare wooden bench. "but I forgot how it is. He has done it to me again. I think that I cannot bear it."

"But, now you know what the specks are." I protested.

"Oh yes," he said, "but I still do not know anything. The answer only made another question. He has done it to me over and over again, and each time I forget. I see, and I strive, and I look, and when finally I get an answer, it becomes another question."

I was totally lost. "Whatever do you mean."

"Why?" he asked emphatically, raising both arms up to the sky as if he were holding something cupped in his hands. "Why would the ants carry another bug up a plant in the morning, and down the plant in the evening? Why would they fight to the death for such a prize when they could eat it for themselves?" He looked to me and shrugged. "I am always left asking, why?"

I lowered my eyes and looked away. I didn't have a clue to offer him. My other teachers always answered my questions.

Then he was laughing, again. By the time I looked back to him, he was dancing his jig again. He was singing and chanting at the same time. "You are awesome. You are so awesome. You are great and I do not deserve to know who you are. You have captured me and I will gladly seek your mysteries until I die. There is nothing to know outside of you. Make yourself known to me. I love you. Oh, I love you." Things like that.

As I listened to him chant, I saw again why some people considered him a little off.

Then, he was back at the microscope examining the tiny speck again.

"All the parts are there." he said thoughtfully. "It's just a bug, a tiny helpless bug. I don't think it could walk across a leaf in a day."

"Master," I injected holding up the magnifying glass, "I think that the specks are big enough to look at with this. We will be able to go right up to the bush and watch."

"That's wonderful!" he exclaimed, "Let's look at the rest of the wonders first."

As we looked at each, I related the place or plant they came from. I found myself being scientific, making observations. The Master had comments for each, also. He was like a child visiting a long awaited place. He laughed and danced, again, to the point where I became uncomfortable. I could understand his joy to a degree, but I was not used to adults acting in such an unrestrained manner. Several times, I tried to calm him down, but each new revelation would rekindle his joy.

When we were finished, he came to me like a child. His eyes gleamed with gratitude. You are like your grandfather. You have given me more than I could ever pay back. I thank you. He shook my hand. It was a business man's handshake, but his eyes were filled with warmth. He exuded thanks.

"You are your grandfather," he said. "You are my friend."

The moment left me confused. I was caught, again, in that horrible bind, not knowing if I was a child or a man.

CHAPTER 8

Once again, the Master did not allow me to wallow too long in my predicament.

"Let us walk," he said. "We have a mystery to solve." Then he laughed. "We have a question to ask, but we do not know what it will be until we solve the mystery."

Changing the subject completely, he asked me what I knew of Great Britain. In a few minutes I found myself in the unwitting role of a lecturer once again. It was one subject my father had discussed with me at length. Father was convinced that the whole world would be well served to live and do business under one ruler. He considered that only a country so tiny and lightly populated could fulfill the role. Father reasoned that England did not have enough people to spread all round the world; therefore, it was forced to allow the native peoples of its colonies to prosper and have entry into the economic development of a nation and a region. I described, at some length, the rise of the monarchy and it's evolution into a representative monarchy. Then I explained the rise of mercantilism and its promise of a world of prosperity. The Master was very impressed. He questioned and commented freely as I orated.

We were in the tall grasses again. I did not remember walking there. It was as if the ideas and words that passed between us had picked us up and deposited us on the Flood Road.

The Master was pointing to a bush ahead. "That's a good one!" he said excitedly. He hurried me along, asking me twice if I was sure I had the magnifying glass in my bag. The ants were there, just as he predicted. I pulled out the magnifying glass and tried to hand it to him, but he would not take it.

"No," he said, "you look and tell me what you see." but, when I moved to position myself, he crowded in close behind me trying to see over my shoulder.

"What do you see?" he whispered impatiently.

"Not much," I replied somewhat uncertainly, not being at all sure what I was supposed to be looking for. "The little specks are all the same. I am pretty sure that they are called aphids. They look as though they can barely move. The ants pick them up and carry them. I have seen two ants pick up and move aphids that looked like they were trying to walk. It looks like the aphids are eating the plant. I can see several whose heads are buried in the soft flesh of the plant."

An exalted shout rose into the air behind me.

"Yes! I knew it! I knew it!"

The Master had become a child again. He was dancing a jig behind me, stamping and dragging his feet in a circle.

"I knew they were farmers." he celebrated. "I knew it."

"What do you mean, farmers?" I asked, looking through the glass trying to imagine what he could possibly mean.

"I was sure that the ants did not eat the plants. They carry the specks to the plant in the morning." he explained. "They carry them down to their homes at the end of the day. They must be farmers."

"Perhaps, they fatten the aphids up during the day and eat some every night in their den," I ventured.

"That is an excellent guess," he said. "What was it you called such a guess?"

"Scientists call them hypothesis," I said with renewed interest in my subject. I was impressed with the realization that we were, indeed, being scientists.

At that moment, I noticed an ant sweeping up an armful of a clear colorless liquid. The ant turned and raced down the stalk with his burden. I noticed others, doing the same thing. All the ants going down the stem carried a small droplet, and each ant climbing the stem was empty.

"Master," I said, "the ants are carrying something down the stem, but I cannot tell what it is."

He moved in closer behind and almost crowded me into the bush. "Can you see where they are getting it? Is it oozing from the wounds in the stem?"

I moved my attention back to the aphids. I found two of the tiny creatures, side by side. Each of them had a tiny clear droplet extruding from their abdomens.

"Euugh!"

"What is it?" demanded the Master, pressing in again on my shoulder, until I nearly lost my balance.

"It is excrement." I said with disappointment, still recoiling at my discovery. "The ants are only removing excrement."

"Of course! Of course!" came a joyful cry behind me. I did not turn around, but I heard his feet stamping into the ground behind and then being dragged about. By that time I could recognize the rhythm of his jig and knew that it was his happy dance.

"Master," I said, "they must be removing it for sanitary purposes."

"No! No!" he insisted. "They eat it."

Eager to prove my point, I examined the ants on their trek down the stem. "No Master, they are simply carrying the droplets down the stem."

"Of course!" he continued, "They are taking it back to their barn for storage."

"What do you mean barn?" I asked with sarcasm coming into my voice. Fear began to rise up in me, that I had just become the victim of some sort of elaborate joke, the kind that adults so often play upon children. I needn't have worried. It was totally out of the Master's character to make fun of anything, but himself.

"They are farmers." he said, beaming. "They do what farmers do."

"Master, please. I know that I am young and that I have said many foolish things to you, but please do not make fun of me in my gullibility."

"No . . No . . No." he said very seriously. "You do not understand. I mean everything I say.

Think about farmers and what they do. Then think about what we know about these ants. They bring the specks out in the morning to graze just as a farmer tends his herd. Farmers protect their animals from predators just as the ants protect their specks from the beetles."

"But Master," I intruded, "we do not eat the excrement of our cattle."

"That is true," he said, "but we do milk them, and we drink the milk. Is milk anything but a by-product of the plant the cow eats? The ants must put the specks on the plant in the morning and protect them from the beetles through the day. The specks are their cows. In return for protecting the specks, the ants get to use the excrement to live and feed their young in some way or another. They are farmers, then." He shrugged as if he was victorious in his reasoning.

"But Master," I insisted, "a farmer thinks and plans.

He is not anything like an ant."

"Perhaps it is the other way around." smiled the Master. "Perhaps a farmer does what he does naturally, because that is what a farmer does. Perhaps the thinking part is only in the human farmer's mind."

"We are more than insects." I insisted.

"True." he said, "The insect does not study us. The ants are not aware that we are here, unless perhaps we would try to rob them of their specks. We, on the other hand, are free to ponder upon them. That is what is unfair."

"What is unfair?" I responded, now fully confused. "You have solved your mystery. Now you know why they do what they do."

"Indeed," he said, "but the greater mystery is ever before me. Why do I wonder? Why must I watch? Why can I watch?

Does the tree wonder after its children, once the seed pods have dropped away from the branch? No! The children of the tree must only hope that the wind drives them far enough away from their mother to survive.

Does the tree consider which birds have nested in its branches? I think not.

It is not that way for me. It seems that my sole purpose in life is to ask, 'Why?' And then, there is another question that follows immediately. 'Who?'

Who designed all this? I cannot imagine that the ants conspire with the specks against the beetles, or that the specks sought out the ants for protection. Who set all this in place?

Let me watch them for a moment."

The Master examined the spectacle. Short sounds of satisfaction escaped him as he watched. "It is awesome." he said.

I was beginning to grow a little bored, but he watched

on for several minutes. At times, it was like he was visiting with old friends. He talked to them like he knew them. Finally, he stood straight and stepped back toward me. He was beaming.

"You have made me a happy man." he said. "I am, at once, ready to die and anxious to go on. The search is endless, but it is a continually new joy." He grabbed me by the shoulders and examined me like he had done the day we met; then he hugged me.

"You ARE your grandfather." he beamed.

We walked again. We talked about anything and everything. I found myself ever in the roll of a lecturer. How could I know so much and still be so incredibly ignorant? Yet, I could not avoid the role. I had an answer for his every question, and I fed on his approval.

We discussed the gods, or god, or whatever, again, but his attitude was different than the day before. He stayed lighthearted and he was able to dance around every question I tried to ask. I realized what was happening, but found myself unable to do anything about it.

The city and the sun were merging as we walked into town. When we arrived at his house, I noticed that the second chicken was gone from the cage. I was invited to join them, again, for the evening meal. Of course, I declined again and made a mental note to have Faude cage up four more chickens to bring with me the next day. Perhaps that would encourage them to cook enough to feed everyone well.

As I left, my stomach, which had been strangely absent from my body through the day, began to knot itself. It urged me to move more quickly to the full table waiting for me at home.

On my way, an odd thought crossed my mind. It seemed like I had two lives. The second life began with the Master. Though it had only been three days, this new life was rich and full of promise to me.

CHAPTER 9

The new day carried me back to the Master's door. I did not know what the day would bring, but I was anxious to find out. We walked out of town wondering about Calcutta. He had never been there, either, and both of us considered what wonders awaited me there.

When we came to the turn off onto the Flood Road, I continued down it absently. My attention was completely on my lecture. I continued, perhaps, twenty paces before I realized the Master had stopped.

"What's wrong?" I said turning around.

"Today, it will be a little different." he said slowly. "Today, you will go on alone. I will wait for you at my home and we will talk there. I will be so interested in what you have found."

Suddenly, a new reality flooded over me. 'Go on alone.' What purpose could that bring? I stood there, lost in the moment. The days had been so good. Who knew what this new day might bring? The days had been so rich for me; there were so few of them left. I truly desired to spend them with him. Why should we waste them?

But, he was adamant. "No. You go on. We will have plenty of time to talk later."

By then, my heart was pounding. I did not wish to

go on alone. I was like a lawyer, suddenly touched by my cause.

"You must go with me." I argued.

"It is necessary that I do not." he said with kind authority. I knew that he understood what I was going through, but that realization did little to comfort me.

"Master," I stammered. "You know the wilds, and I do not."

"That may be true," he said, "but I have cautioned you about all you need to be aware of. If I continue to show you only what I know, you will not find anything out for yourself. Soon, you will go to Calcutta, alone. You must do this."

Once I thought about Calcutta, I stopped arguing. He was right; though, I could not imagine it, death and danger must be there, too. I had learned enough from the Master to see his point.

"It will be all right," he said reassuringly.

I stood there, alone, with my back to the unknown road. My head hung down low on my chest. Once again, the precocious young man was a helpless child. The core of my being shrunk smaller and smaller. I felt his hand on my shoulder, but it felt as though it only touched the shell of me. His hand was still a long way from me. There was a void between us.

"You must." he whispered. "It is the next lesson."

I could not look at him when I turned to walk. This was now a question of manhood, a test, not a lesson. I would pass the test. I passed tests.

CHAPTER 10

My resolve carried me out of his sight, and then some, but my mind measured each step I took. Each step took me measurably away from my life, and into a separate life that belonged to someone or something else. That life did not recognize my father, much less me. I felt naked. That nakedness was magnified by the realization that I had clothes on. Nothing here cared anything about whether I was clothed or not, only if I was there to eat, or be eaten.

The thought made me hollow. I saw the remains of a body, in my mind. The bones and ribs were bleached in the sun and spread apart in a circle. It was me! Once the tiger had his full of me, all that was left were bones. They were fought over and pulled apart by the small meat eaters and the birds. Each vertebrae of my spine lay separated by the birds fighting for a beak full of the leftovers, anything that the larger animals could not tear or lick away.

I almost vomited as the picture passed through my mind. My life was a meaningless commodity, and each step I took made it worth less.

Suddenly, I was aware only of my body. A few seconds before, it had been an empty shell. Now, I was filled with myself.

Life pulsed through every fiber of my being. The sides of my head were being crushed by the flow of the blood in my veins. My ears sought comfort from the pounding cacophony, but I could not turn anything off. My whole body shook with each mighty beat of my heart. The sun grew distant and alien before my eyes. My lungs heaved air wildly in and out and raced against themselves. Death came and covered me with a covering that smothered every inch of my skin. I thought I would pass out at any second. My skin grew cold and tried to shrink, but it was unable to compress any of my inner functions. They were flying out of control, independent of each other.

In the next instant, a silence came. My racing mind felt the smallest moment of relief, before the awful turnabout became evident to me. My pounding heart had stopped beating and begun to race. It doubled its beat, and then doubled it again, and again. I could tell that it stopped beating entirely. It quivered helplessly in the middle of my chest, giving no opportunity for blood to enter or leave. At once, I was deaf to everything that happened outside my body, and prey to everything happening within it.

My knees began to buckle and I knew that I would be on the ground if I did not act. It was a time for action! So, I ran. I ran back, back to the main road.

Flushed as it was with energy my body reacted as though it were a perfect machine. Every stride was strong. Every step was sure. My lungs were grateful for the purpose my legs gave them. I felt like I was being pushed along, effortlessly, and I ran like a wind.

The intersection of the roads reached out to me, as

I entered it. I felt the arms of safety reach out and pull me into a soft embrace. I stopped in the center of the opening and held myself by the knees. The air rushing into my lungs was now a sweet breath of life. My heart began to slow down with some semblance of rhythm. I was alive fully, absolutely, completely alive. As the richness of that realization crept over me, I raised myself.

It was then that I saw the Master. He sat on the ground in the shade only a few steps away. My panicked state did not allowed me to notice anything but the prize, as I raced to save myself.

Shame and guilt rolled over me like separate waves. I experienced each with one devastating conclusion. I was a failure. And more, I would always be a failure. This would be my last lesson. The Master would rise up and rebuke my weakness. I was not his best student, but his biggest failure. I had failed the test. He would report my worthlessness to my father. I was not even the shadow of my grandfather.

He rose with obvious labor, and slowly moved toward me. I waited for his voice to break the silence with my head down. My only question was whether his voice would be filled with pity or disdain.

"I have been waiting for you." he said innocently. "You must have fought the battle well."

"You knew!" I cried hoarsely. "You knew I would come back."

"Let us just say that I assumed." he smiled, without a hint of judgment. Imperceptibly, he began to walk down the Flood road; unknowingly, I began to walk after him.

"It was necessary." he began. "I had to see how you would react."

Anger began to filter itself into my emotions. I saw myself the object of his humor. Incredibly, I did not notice that we were walking on the same road I had just run down. It was the Master's way, his gift, if you will.

"What happened?" he asked with an innocence that irritated me even more.

"You know very well what happened to me." I shot back. "You said you were waiting for me."

"Well yes," he confessed, "but, have you ever asked a traveler in town how he arrived? Almost everyone comes upstream, but there are still many possibilities about the circumstances that bring them. I am asking you to relate to me the sequence of events that led you to run into the opening."

I told him everything about the flush of emotions and symptoms I experienced. At first, it seemed that there was nothing to remember, but the panic. As I talked, I began to understand a little about what had transpired.

I was alone and helpless. I took the most appropriate steps to deal with my situation. My recitation began to take on the aura of a lawyer, again, making his argument for the defense. As I spoke, I began to convince myself of something. If I could say the right words, perhaps I could change my guilt into innocence.

The Master looked at me and smiled.

"Why is it different, now?" he asked, looking around.

I followed his eyes and saw that we were almost across the Flood Road.

"It must be you Master. You would not allow harm to come to me."

He began to laugh. It was a silly laugh, directed more at himself than my ignorance. "What harm am I strong enough to deliver us from?" he asked thoroughly amused.

"You know the wilds." I said. "You know the cobra,

and hunt with him. You know the tiger by his stripes and his prints in the mud. You said so yourself. You see danger for what it is."

"Still, I cannot defend you from the unknown." he argued. "I will gladly tell you that I will offer myself to death to spare you. I owe that much, and more, to your grandfather. I would be dead already if it were not for him."

"Yes, but you know much more than I. You would not allow harm to come to me."

"You could have died today." he said with a sudden coldness. "Do you know when the chances were the best?"

"The moment I stepped alone onto the flood road." I shot back, trying to make him feel a little guilty. "I am a city boy. I do not know the animals and the dangers of the wilds."

"Your reasoning is correct," he replied, "but my question was, 'What moment were you in the greatest danger?'"

"The danger increased with each step I took into the unknown. I was walking into a world where I did not belong."

"What was the danger, then, at the moment that you turned and ran?" He was insisting that I give him an answer, when I was not sure one existed.

"It was not an exact thing. I recognized my danger. You, yourself, said I did well to have gone as far as I did alone."

"But my point," he replied, still pressing me, "is, what was the danger, and when were you the most susceptible to it? Did the danger decrease when you turned?"

"No, I guess not." I replied. "I remember when I tried to talk you into going back the other day and you told me the tiger could be in waiting behind us, but I did not think about that. Everything in my being told me that I had to do something, escape to the closest, easiest place of safety. At that moment, safety seemed to be back on the River Road. I didn't have to think anymore. My fear made me beyond thinking."

"What was that? What did the fear do to you?" he demanded.

"Master, I was so afraid, I thought I would die!" I exclaimed, helpless again.

"What did you say about the fear?" he insisted. "When were you the most vulnerable?"

"When I stopped thinking," I mumbled, but I failed to see any great revelation.

"Indeed." he said stopping. He put his hands firmly on my shoulders. "Now consider this, can you ever be more vulnerable than when you stop thinking, especially if you stop thinking and run? Do you remember the cobra we encountered? What if you had run into him? Surely, you would be dead at this moment. So, the real danger came . . . " he paused and allowed me to finish his thought.

"When I took action without thinking," I said, seeing some sense in his questioning.

"That's not exactly what I was driving at." he said. "Can you think of an instance were such an instantaneous, unthinking reaction would be called for?"

"I suppose it would be called for if I almost walked over the snake. Any means of escape would be acceptable, once I knew what to escape from."

"Precisely!" he exalted closing his fist in may face. "Can you see that recognizing the potential for danger is entirely different from recognizing the danger? The first is so important, but it's meaningless unless you follow through."

"Master, you are trying to get me to say that I was in the greatest danger when I was running to save myself, aren't you?"

He smiled meekly.

"I could not say it for you, because you have to see it that way for yourself. You see, you are advanced.

As you live your life, you will see many people fleeing a danger they suppose to be there; their catastrophe will be waiting for them in the midst of their flight. Some people seem to live their whole lives like they are trying to escape from danger."

"You make life sound hopeless, Master. I fear that I am one of those people. I ran from something I imagined. I am not sure I will ever face a situation like that without running."

His laughter disarmed me.

"Do you consider that makes you different? In reality, it joins you together with the rest of us."

"You mean that all people are subject to these frailties?" I asked, thinking specifically of my father. I never saw him react to any situation out of fear. Even when Mother died, he seemed to be the master of his pain.

"My experience has shown me that all people experience moments when they are stressed to a breaking point. Fear is only one of the demons which attacks us. Anger and envy will also bring similar despair, but I consider them to be like younger cousins of fear. I think they get some of their strength from fear, too."

"Then what sense is there in anything?" I sighed. "I will never escape from a fear like today's."

"Oh, I would never wish such a fate upon you." he replied quickly. "I have encountered many cobras. Do you think that I would encourage you to pretend that the cobra was harmless?"

I was no longer sure of anything, except that I did

not want to walk the road alone. "I know that you would not suggest that, but I am confused." Once again I hung on that endless string of childhood, unable to climb up and bewildered by my predicament.

"Suppose I suggest that fear could be more appropriately viewed in terms of time?" he suggested. "That is to say, could there be a right time for fear and a wrong time?"

The question intrigued me. I always thought of fear in terms of things, some *thing* to be afraid of. "I suppose there is something to say for that." I pondered, going along with the thought. "I have heard of people being afraid of the river. In reality, the river would only be something to fear if your boat was sinking, or if it was in flood stage."

"Exactly!" chimed in the Master. "The river and railroad are responsible for the prosperity of our town. Most of the time the river is our friend. Since you put it that way, I remember before you were born, some people were afraid of the railroad. One man said the town would sink into the river with the weight of the train. Another man said the noise would stop the rice seeds from sprouting. It all proved unfounded, but let that train go off its track while coming at you, and you better choose to fear and run very quickly." We both laughed at the thought.

As we walked, I formed the principles that have guided me through my life. I did not realize it at the time, but the ideas we shared on that walk were proved to me over and over again.

I cannot tell you the number of times that cold paralyzing fear rose up to control me. It came in different forms. Sometimes, it screamed for me to flee. At other times, fear demanded action against some threat or enemy before they could mount their attack. There were those times when my whole future was clouded by sure failure. It was inescapable and complete, and it was fear.

As I grew older I became able to recognize fear by its personality, its face, if you will. I trace the beginning of my revelation to that day, that walk, and that talk.

Before I was aware of it, another day was gone. We had walked over the Flood Road again, and the evening was an unwelcome, ill-timed visitor, who forced his way into my life.

CHAPTER 11

Only three chickens remained in the crate at his hut. It appeared that these people refused to allow me to influence their consumption.

I found myself thinking of Faude and Silke as family. Today, I would race home to share my day with them.

After I finished recounting the days event to them, Faude assured me. "The Master is correct. I am getting older and I can identify fear as our main enemy. It waits for our weakness and rises then, to overpower us. It never attacks without a weakness to aim at, and death is our inevitable weakness."

We talked for several hours. It reminded me of when Mother was alive. I slept with a comfort remembered from days long passed. It felt good and complete. I knew the new day would take me back to the Flood Road. Failure seemed to wait for me there, but that was a problem for another day.

The Master was waiting as I approached. His eyes studied me head to toe. We both knew what awaited me, even though we had not discussed it the day before.

Today was my day to go through the flood road alone.

We both knew it.

"Have you prepared yourself?" he asked without emotion.

"I am not sure." I said, looking to him for some direction.

"That is an excellent answer." The words bubbled out of him. His upper body started to sway back and forth. I was afraid, for a moment, he would start to dance his jig, again. Thankfully, he did not. It did not seem possible that my answer could have been that good.

He began enthusiastically, "I have noticed that the people who are the most sure of what will happen are wrong the most often. So you see, you have given a truly good answer. You will not know what you will do until after the moment of decision comes to you, wherever and whenever that happens.

Do you think there will be anything different today?"

"Today, I know that I will be afraid. Even at this moment I am afraid, for I know the fear that waits for me."

"Excellent! Excellent!" he sang. Now he was jigging. "You don't cover yourself with false pride." He stopped dancing and moved very close to me, pointing his aging finger into the center of my chest. "You may not walk the Flood Road alone, today. But, you will!"

"How can you be so confident in my ability?" I asked.

"It does not have anything to do with my confidence in you, which is very high any way." he said. "Forgive me, but it is my confidence in man. You have been over the Flood Road three or four times, now. The reason I know you will be successful lies in your familiarity with the road. You have been down the road with me, and now you know the way. That is why you will be successful."

"Yes." I interjected, "but I have been with you."

"I knew the way, and now, you do too. Do you think I could protect you from any real danger?" he asked, exaggerating the point by showing me the weakness of his arms and legs. "I am at the door of death."

"Your wisdom and knowledge protected me from the cobra." I reasoned.

"Indeed, I knew what to look for and where to look, but so do you, now, unless you run like you did yesterday. You cannot see much when you run."

"Master, I still cannot see the value in it." I said, hoping somehow to gain a reprieve.

"Let me ask you a question." he paused and looked me squarely in the eye. "I am not sure it will come in Calcutta, but I am sure that the day will come that you will be as afraid as you were yesterday."

The very thought of returning to that fear caused my stomach to turn. The fingers of fear began to reach into my chest and pull on my heart and lungs.

"I think, that I will die if that happens. I will burst and my inners will fly out."

"Be that as it may," he continued, "you will come to a place like that again. Perhaps, it will be today on the road. My question is, 'What will you think in the moment before you take action?'"

"If that same moment comes I will flee without a thought." I assured him.

"Well," he said with finality, "how will we know, unless you go, . . . alone?"

"What would you have me to think?" I asked helplessly. "Tell me and I will work very hard to learn the right way to think, and perhaps in two or three days . . ."

"I guess, I would only want you to ask yourself whether running was the best thing." he interrupted me innocently.

"I promise you, Master, I will try not to run back today."

"Oh, No!" he protested, "What if running is what you should do? Don't you see? I cannot tell you what the best thing to do might be, because I will not be there. You will have to be your own advisor in that moment."

I began to cry. They were the tears of a child. I was again a helpless child and every answer I had seemed to be wrong.

"Perhaps I should not go at all." I said. I did not say it in anger, but the emotion was starting to rise within me.

"Why should I expose myself to these things at all. I think that I should avoid them at all cost. It seems stupid to me to choose to go into danger."

"But, you have been down the road with me." he insisted. "Will you live the rest of your life in Kenshi? Or, better yet, will you live the rest of your life in your father's house?" His words were insistent, but not mocking. The tone of his voice told me that I had to insist that the answer was, 'no'.

"You will not experience the same fear today, because you know that it is coming." he said, so surely that I thought he was looking into the future. "You will see fear coming on the horizon of your soul; you do, even now. You will point to it as it comes near you. You will call out to it, and when you do, you will challenge it."

I interrupted him. I felt completely helpless, and he was speaking as though I had some kind of authority. I knew that, whatever it was, I did not possess it. I was quite sure I never could. "Master, you do not know what happened to me yesterday."

"Perhaps," he smiled patiently, "you do not know the nature of fear. You do not have to conquer it. You only have to recognize it. When you speak to it, it will freeze in its tracks."

"Master, you are speaking of fear as though it is an animal."

"Perhaps," he nodded, "but perhaps, fear is more like a thief. He comes and takes everything he can get away with, but once you see a thief, he either runs away, or he pretends that he is your friend. Fear will advise you as long as you recognize him. The important question is do you want to take his advice."

"My father is an honorable man." I said. "He seeks honorable men, not thieves to be his advisors."

"Your father has walked a road alone." he said smiling. "It was not the Flood Road, but it was close."

"Did my father go through the first time, alone?" I asked.

"It is unimportant," he said, sensing that I would talk about anything to avoid going on. We were at the fork, which led off across the delta into the grasses. "We can discuss that later, but I really think you should ask your father to tell you about it."

His hands were on my shoulders. They held me and at the same time each gesture that passed through his arms was a part of the send off, a preparation for my going out.

"Master, I do not think I can do this." I said weakly.

"In that case, we will walk together again." he reassured me. "First, you must make the attempt and then we will talk, either at my house or on the road, it makes no difference."

With a final gesture of firmness, he turned me.

CHAPTER 12

There was no pretense in my walk that day. I had already failed the test, and another failure waited for me just around the first bend.

I did not go very far before an odd notion struck me. I wanted to see how the Master chose to wait for me. I turned carefully and crept back to a place where I could see the intersection, but I could not see him anywhere. Then I became concerned that he was hidden and watching me. Carefully, I moved into another position. It was only then that I saw him in the distance. He was almost out of sight, headed back toward Kenshi.

From the distance, I could see that he was going to die soon. I know that sounds strange, but I could see it. He was so tiny. His movements were slow and labored. Still, he moved back and forth from bush to tree, tree to bush. It seemed that he intended to greet and inspect each living thing on the path. It was silly for me to consider that he brought me any safety, but he did. I have found over the years that there is safety in wisdom, even when it is not imposing.

Today, he was not waiting for me. "He must know I

am going to pass through." I thought. I only wished I could be so sure.

So, I began again. I measured my steps. I would walk, a short firm solid step, but each step would be forward.

My mind stayed numb to any thought until I reached the point of my defeat the day before. I saw it coming up before me. Somehow, I was safe right up to the point of my progress the previous day. A wall waited for me there. It was invisible, but I knew that if I tried to walk through it my legs would become stuck in some invisible goo and I would be easy prey for the smallest of the predators watching, invisible from their hiding spots all around me.

They would bite and rip my flesh in small, agonizing bits. It would be better to perish in the single powerful crush of the tiger.

My breathing began to be erratic, as I stood over the invisible line. I heard my heart join in, in a rhythmic sort of a song. It was as if they were instruments in a band, and I was the only one who could hear.

I do not know how long I stood there. I tried to think. I remembered the Master's words. I would see fear on the horizon of my soul. I saw fear everywhere. Every shadow was a hidden enemy. Every sound in the bush was the unwary step of a confident hunter moving slowly in for an easy kill.

My dilemma became very simple. I knew that I was going to fail, again, but I could not fail without taking at least one step more than the day before. I could not go back without that one step to measure from.

The step came without a decision. It simply happened. The wall was different than I imagined. It still seemed to be there, but the miring goo was not in evidence. Rather, I felt the skin on my leg tighten preparing that leg to act; every muscle was tight and prepared to go into motion.

The second step was a test. I had to see if the ground would give way and suck me in. As soon as I took the step, both my limbs informed my body that they were ready. Nothing changed in the world around me, but inside me a silent chorus rose up. It demanded another step, and then another. I did not think, but I did walk.

With each step my resolve grew to take another. Soon there was a cacophony inside me, demanding that I run with the wind, but forward this time. My mind demanded that my body give my eyes the time to search the next few steps ahead. "I must not run," I told my body, "otherwise the cobra will not know that I am not trying to eat him and kill me defending himself."

I had to use all of my willpower to control my body, but soon I was focused completely, on the next step. My eye covered every meter of my path. No step was made until the way was cleared by my eye, and then by my mind. Still each step was sure and quick, and each step took me one step closer to my goal. Soon I was clearing the next three steps, but I still had to hold on to the control of my legs. They pulled and strained to break into a faster gait, anything to reach the goal.

My body began to thank me for the movement, becoming fully operational. My ears searched into the underbrush for any sound that did not belong. My nose examined every passing scent. But, I went on. This time, I was unable to stop. It did not matter what I thought I heard or smelled. There was no question of what I would do or which way I would go. I would go forward. Today, forward was the only way I would go. Humorously, the thought crossed my mind several times, that going forward was not that much superior to going backward.

It still felt a little like failure.

At least I was doing something, so I walked.

Soon I began to recognize landmarks that told me I was growing closer to safety. My assurance rose. Retreat was no longer an option, safety was ahead, only ahead. I could not go back anymore.

It seemed that victory would rise up and welcome me home, but it did not. I reached the river road again, and I was not a failure; still, I did not experience any satisfaction in my victory.

CHAPTER 13

The Master said we would talk after my walk. As I began walking along the river back to the city, I tried to review my experiences in preparation for that report, but there was nothing to report.

He was sitting in the shade of a giant tree that covered six or seven of the huts and an intersection of streets. Many people were enjoying the shade and the trickle of a breeze it provided, some were venders, others were just gossiping. I noticed how common he looked. I could not tell him apart from the rest of the poor, who surrounded him. My dress gave me away as an outsider. I was not comfortable there at all.

Thankfully, he started to rise as soon as he saw me coming. His broad smile was full of expectation. I could tell that he expected a long detailed recounting of my experiences and observations. It surprised me, that I had a strong inclination to make something up.

He motioned for me to follow him and led me between the walls of the huts to another tree off the street, There were still people there, but not the amount of activity of the first tree. We would be able to talk there in privacy.

"Well, Well," he said still smiling broadly, "I can see

that you were successful, . . . but I can also see that you are not happy about something. What happened? Is something wrong?"

"Not exactly." I said lowering my head. "I tried to think of something to report to you, but nothing happened except for the moment when I had to take one step beyond where I stopped yesterday. Other than that, nothing happened."

"Well, tell me about that." he chortled, obviously quite satisfied with the expectation. I was immediately ashamed of myself for considering lying to him. I should have known that he would be happy with whatever happened and he would be able to see something in it, so I began. I told him how I had turned back and tried to see what he was doing. I remembered the confidence I had gained from watching him as he walked back towards home and thanked him for helping my resolve. He laughed when I recalled how he went from bush to tree and back, like a man making his way through a crowd of old acquaintances, but I did not tell him that I saw that he would die soon.

"I had a feeling that you would be successful today." he smiled.

"Master, you said my father walked a road, too. Must all your students do this? How many made it through the first day?"

"You ask too many questions." he laughed. "I am the one condemned to a life full of questions, besides it is never the same. Each student is different. In the old days I was the only teacher in this town. Your grandfather bought me my house. He sent your father to me for years and paid me to teach him. My days of labor were spent reaching into the minds of young men, because your grandfather encouraged the other more prominent people to send their sons to me.

Kenshi was a small trading village before the English picked it to be the source of the railroad to the highland plateaus. There was little need for an education here before the railroad came. If you could count to ten, you could do business."

"Was my grandfather really a great man?" I wondered.

"You are asking the questions, again." he scolded, laughing as he spoke. "It is my job to ask questions, and your job to answer them."

"Master, you have not given me anything to study. Teachers lecture or supply their students with study material. How can you expect your students to answer questions when they have not been given the answers to learn?"

"You See! You're asking them, again!" he said laughing uproariously and rocking back and forth. I laughed with him, but once again, I was not sure exactly where the humor lay.

"Your grandfather was a great man to me." he said, solemn and humble again, before I was done laughing. "When I went to work for him he understood my malady, my sickness, immediately. I could work very hard, doing whatever needed to be done, but I had to ask why. I had to ask others why. When I asked him why he ran his business in certain ways, he answered me. That in itself made him great to me. He did not have to answer my questions, but he did.

After a few months he called me in to talk to him. For a moment I thought he was going fire me for being bothersome, and asking too many questions; but instead, he said, 'You are a strange man. You ask me questions and as I answer them I find better ways to run my business. It would be a simple matter if it only happened once, but it has happened often. I'm afraid I must increase your responsibilities and allow you to question all my employees.'

Your grandfather gave me authority over his entire business. At that time your father was only three or four years old. I worked for your grandfather for two years as his manager. He traveled the river on the steamships and his business grew greatly. Then the day came, when he summoned me, again.

'I do not know what to do with you,' he said. 'The railroad is coming to Kenshi soon, and you have given me many workers who cry out for a challenge and more responsibility. Several could perform your job very adequately. So I must change your assignment. From now on you must teach my son to read and reason.'

So you see, he set me free. He gave me the fondest desire of my heart, a desire I did not allow myself to dream. He let me be a teacher." The Master lowered his head and looked away, but I still saw his eyes flush full with tears.

"You were the last debt." he said. "I promised him, that I would teach you if I lived.

So, now comes the test. What have I taught you?" He looked at me and waited, as if expecting an answer.

Many things passed through my mind. First, I thought of the steam engine and science, but I was the one who lectured him on those subjects. I was the one who presented my information about economics, business, and history.

"I do not know for sure Master, but rest assured, you have taught me. I am different, and I am more than I was only days ago."

"I have seen that in this conversation," he assured me, "for I see you doing the only thing I know how to do, ask questions. I am joyfully irritated that you do not give me a chance to ask my questions before you fill the air with yours. Can you see any value in that?" he laughed.

"I think so," I said, "in school they taught us that a scientist's first job is to ask questions. But, didn't you say asking questions was your curse?"

"You're doing it again." he laughed in mock anger. "It only seems like a curse when I am stuck on the end of it. As I pursue my questions I see so many things besides the answer.

It is that pursuit which drives me. It makes my life complete. I desire nothing but my answer, and so I live. Each answer becomes a new question. How can I die?"

He was laughing, again. It looked like he was going to get up and dance, so I thought quickly.

"How can questions be so important?" I asked. "In school I have struggled to learn answers."

"There you go!" he exclaimed, wagging a finger at me, "Putting me on the spot, again.

Consider for a moment what my goals might be for you. If I were to try to teach you something in these few days, what could I possibly teach you? You may learn mathematics and history, but those are not primary things to me, nor is there time. But, oh," he wished, "if I could teach you to question without frustration, then, I would be complete. Unfortunately, I do not know how to do that. I don't really think anyone does, not even the high minded and prideful experts. I have run into a few of them. You will, too. I hope that you never become like them. I think they make it a practice to ask questions they already know the answers to and avoid everything else. How convenient is that? What challenge is there in that?"

"Until I met you," I confessed, "I only considered that I would become a business man. I know that my father wants me to follow after him, but now I am not sure what I want to do. I'm not even sure I want to go to Calcutta to school."

"What would you do," he laughed, "stay here with me? I have very little left to teach you. You are so advanced."

"If I would tell you the truth," I said looking down, "you might not think of me as so advanced."

"Exactly what do you mean." he said, moving a little closer to me, so that I could whisper and still be heard.

"I am a child," I confessed, "so many times I think I am moving forward into manhood and then something will happen. It has happened often with you. Something will happen and I will be slapped in the face by the truth. I am still a pathetic helpless child and I feel like I will always be a helpless child. Nothing can change that."

I did not have a chance to say more. His ancient limbs began to move at once, dancing even as he labored to get up. He shouted and danced in some sort of victory celebration. It did not seem to have anything to do with the confession I'd just made. He waved his arms and made swinging gestures with his hands, while his feet stamped the ground emphatically every third step.

I sat there, lost, until he came back to me. His eyes were big and wide.

"Never!" He wagged his finger in my face sternly, "Never, forget that!" His voice grew quiet and serious. He moved close to me and measured his words out to me as though they were gold, and he did not want any thieves to overhear. "No matter how great you become, no matter how much wealth you accumulate, no matter how many men will lay themselves out prostrate before you, never forget that you are a child."

His eyes filled with tears, and he turned away.

"Master," I whispered, "are you all right?"

He laughed, but he kept himself turned away. The laughter carried tears down his cheeks. "I am a child, too." he whispered in a broken chant. He began to walk away. "Let's go where we can talk alone." he said, and led me to a private shaded area along the river.

"The great God who met me in the wilds, and walked through my life with me, He is a Father. He is the Father of all that is, and I have been given enough to see that I am a child, helpless and in need. I do not even know enough to know what name to call Him."

"I am convinced," he said resolutely, "that I am in ignorance. I have sought after information about every god I have ever heard of, and none of them is the one who whispers to me in the night."

I say He is the Father of all that is, and I speak wrongly. The whisper I hear says that it is the ignorance of man that makes its gods after males and females. 'I am above all the labels that you must put on your gods so that you can understand them and picture them. I am before there was any need for he and she. If you ponder why things are the way they are, you come to me. I am ever before you. Consider the sun as it sets and you consider an image of me. Bend down and squint to see the speck as it is carried by the ant and I wait there to show you part of myself. I wait for you to look. Do not be satisfied with less. Find me in the sky and find me in the earth under your feet.'

I cry out. 'You mock me. My mind is too small. My frame is too frail. I am a man. What is a man before you, but a helpless infant? He shrivels to nothing before you.'

I get angry. I am hurt. I am helpless. That is when I hear him. 'I want you to know me. I desire above all else that you know me.'

So now you know why I cannot teach you anything about religion. I am a crazy old man, driven in every direction. How can I teach you? I seek the truth and I find love. I look into chaos, and find order. I call aloud in my helplessness, and hear the whisper of a great Father. I am a child, a helpless infant, but I have no right to call myself His child. I share the same standing as a tree or a tiger. Even the great river is nothing before Him. Yet of them all, I alone cry out to know Him. I study them and ask them my questions about Him. They do not answer me, but He does. He shows himself to me in them."

"Master, would you have me suffer the same fate as you?" I asked.

"No. Never." he said, "I do not think there are many men called to live a life like mine. I only want to emphasize to you that should never delude yourself into thinking too highly of yourself. Your wisdom should begin with being a child."

"But, I desire to leave this painful predicament behind me." I argued. "How can I willingly continue in something which compels me to overcome?"

"I know. I know." he squealed, "Isn't it awesome? There is One so great that, if you truly strive to measure accurately you will be stuck on one terrible conclusion. You are only a helpless child. Then you strive for more. You strive to know, to become. Once you succeed, you are a child again. He is so awesome, it doesn't matter. It's worth it all."

Tears and laughter were mixed on his face, and I knew that it was not my life he measured, but his own.

Chapter 14

And so it was, that my report of my first day alone on the road carried well into the evening. It seemed impossible to me. I went to the Master thinking that I had nothing to report, and we talked for hours about all the things I did not remember. People came and went. The smells of cooking food wafted in the air from different directions. As it turned out, a flock of birds chose that tree to roost in. They announced the end of the day.

Silke and Faude were waiting for me with a table full of food. They would not eat with me, but stayed at the table. I talked with them for several more hours. It seemed impossible to imagine that we ever allowed our daily conversation to die away, after my mother died.

The morning rushed into my ears the way the day before left, with the raucous noise of birds. They seemed to be singing out a challenge for the day ahead. I thought it strange, since I faced the challenge of my life the day before.

My security broke like a fragile glass, when I remembered that nothing really happened to me the day before. My battle had been inside me. I was not forced to face or flee real danger. Perhaps, this day would bring, not only real danger, but a real end for my life.

As I walked to the Master's house, a plan formed within me. The more I practiced it, the better and more reasonable it became. I traveled the road alone; therefore, there was no need to go alone again. We should proceed together. There was not much time left for us to spend together. The Master said it was so. He said that things were different with each of his students. I thought my plan was foolproof. I was sure that all the arguments he could possibly have could be reasonably answered.

I waited until we were out of town before easing my idea into the conversation. I thought I was ready for any argument, but nothing could have prepared me for his laughter. It said that no discussion was possible, in fact, the concept was unthinkable.

"It would be like building a house," he said, "and not putting a roof on it. Right now, you wouldn't need a roof too badly, because it's not the rainy season. But soon, when the rainy season comes, not having a roof means you do not have a house."

I knew it was hopeless, so I did not bother to continue. The Master acted as though there was no need to discuss it further and chattered away about flowers and trees. The rainy season would begin in earnest in a week or so, and everything would change shortly.

Our region received at least some rain all year long. He showed me that some plants showed the preparation of their wait for an influx of water to flower and reproduce. Others were just casting off their seeds in hopes of a favorable location for a new generation. I knew the proper names of many of them, but the Master introduced them to me as though they were old friends, with nicknames. There was no need for formalities. He introduced me to their oddities and per-

sonalities.
　Before I knew it we were at the fork in the road. I decided to make one last attempt to prevail with my idea.
　"Master, I still think it better that we go on together." I began carefully. "I have been down this road, now. It has nothing new to offer me. You are the one who has taught me more than I could have imagined in only a few days. You still have much to teach me of the wilds."
　"Oh, on the contrary," he said with just a hint of testiness, "you are going to school in that beautiful city of dreams, Calcutta. You will not need to know of the wilds there. Besides, how do you know the road has nothing new to teach you? You have only been down it once. If I said to you that each new day was like a road, would you tell me that it was not worth going through, just because you had traveled through a day twenty-four hours before?"
　I could see it was hopeless, so I walked away.
　"I will be under the tree waiting for you," he called. Something in his voice told me that he was trying to tell me that he would rather be with me, too, but he could not say it.
　My steps carried me smoothly past the critical point of the first day. I was still arguing with myself about the relevance of this walk. Then, I realized that I never thought once about the Master. I never considered turning around, to see what he was doing. Today was just boring. I was walking, because it was not really safe to run, and I had to get to the other end of the road.
　I remembered the cobra and chose my steps more carefully. Then I realized that I was in the tall grasses. The tiger lived in the tall grasses. Just because I did not die yesterday, did not mean that I could not die today. The boredom flew from my mind like a flushed

bird. There was no question that today I would walk the road, but the possibility existed that I would not reach its end.

I felt my body tighten. My muscles became alert, ready to act. My breathing and heart responded, not in a wild way, like the first day. They were under control. The message was simple, "We are ready to act, if you need us."

As I walked, considering the condition of my members, the strangest sensation came upon me. It was as if I was no longer completely in my body. I, the part of me that thought, was stretched to the farthest point that I could see. My ears pierced into the unseen bush and carried a thinking part of me along with them. My nose looked for every opportunity to expand me. It strained to the limits of its ability to discern the differences in the smells that wandered by it.

Two days before, I had been locked in my body, chained inside it, and forced to endure, with it, a fear that ravaged every sense and organ differently.

Today, my skin seemed to become only another way to measure where I was. Other parts of me were far beyond the limits of my skin. If danger did confront me, my survival could hinge solely upon my ability to see beyond myself. So, I strained. I strained every particle of my being to see everything that could be seen. I inclined my ear to reach as far as it could reach.

I saw that fear was not an enemy that could kill me. Fear was the thief, who would rob me of the information needed to identify the danger, which could kill me. That danger most likely walked on legs, or crawled on its belly. It could be waiting in the shadows ahead. If I knew it was there, I had hope.

I walked on scarcely able to believe what had happened to me. I, the part of me that made me a being, existed on several different planes.

Each of my senses stretched me to the limits of their reach. I saw every flicker of every leaf on every bush. My brain examined each to determine which might be unusual, and thus worthy of further study. My ears heard every breaking twig and every rustle in the grasses that surrounded me. Without effort, my mind categorized each sound by many different rationale. My nose allowed me to step beyond the dimension of time, to a degree. The stench of something dead in the grasses alerted me to the violence of another day. Together, they worked in a perfect, balanced harmony. This was how my body was meant to work. This was the way everything that happened to me the first day was supposed to have happened.

This reality carried me through the grasses before mid-morning. The end of the flood road came to me before I was ready. This was a victory! I wanted to savor it a while longer, but I could not make the road longer, and the road was my victory. I conquered it that day. I saw the reason for the Master's insistence. It was a lesson, I could only learn alone. It would be invaluable to me for the rest of my life. I must never let this moment, this awareness, slip away. This was a different type of living. This was being a MAN! I liked the way it felt.

CHAPTER 15

I could not go to the Master fast enough. I found him underneath the same tree we used the previous day. As I sat, I realized I was sweating, not from the heat, from the push within me to find him and report my successes.

"Today, I see satisfaction on you." he said, smiling.

My revelation could not come out quickly enough. I told him what I felt. Then, I told him what I thought. Then, I told him what it meant.

He listened impassionately. He did not ask a question or attempt interrupt me.

Finally, I ended with a profound statement of thanks and respect. I was an ignorant foolish child, and he helped me to take a strong and meaningful step into manhood. I would never question him again. His supposed debt to my grandfather could be counted as paid in full.

I expected him to be satisfied. In my mind, I looked for him to reach out to me with both arms and tell me that I had graduated. I was now, ready for life.

Instead, he put his hand to his mouth. Slowly, a question formed, "But, what happened on your walk? You did not tell me anything that happened."

"I told you everything." I insisted. "This was the greatest day of my life."

"I understand that," he said, patiently, "but, . . . but did nothing happen around you? Were you the only event on the road this day? Did nothing else occur?"

I was irritated and perplexed at once. It was true, I was not aware of anything other than my victory. It was very reasonable to me. How could the Master expect more? Other things shrunk to a lesser significance. I could not honestly imagine how anything could be any different; after all, the road was the same road every day. Everything that happened on it, happened every day. The bushes would flower. The ants and the beetles would fight their daily battles over the white aphids. A cobra or two would venture across the road in pursuit of some rodent. Crossing into manhood happened only once for every man.

"Master, this day . . . this day marks a momentous point in my life. Now, I know. I know fear, and how it seeks to control me. I know what to do. From now on, I know what to do. What more could you hope for me?"

He looked at the ground intently. I thought I saw tears in his eyes.

"I want you to see everything." he said, lifting his eyes to me as tears streamed down his face.

He seemed helpless before me.

"I what you to see everything." he said again. "I don't want anything to escape your mind. I do not want different or less for you. I want more. I want all."

He was so frail and helpless before me. I saw there must be something more, something yet unsaid. Then, I perceived that his helplessness was not for me, but for himself. What he wanted for me was the cry of his heart. His only hope was that I would be infused with his passion.

"I thought you would be thrilled for me." I stammered.

"I am. I am." he answered resolutely. "I only hoped that you would be a little different from me, but you're not. You're just like me."

The way he said it, made it sound like an insult.

"Master," I chided, "what are you trying to teach me, if not the lessons you learned with pain?"

The lightness of his laughter returned as quickly as it left.

"You're doing it again," he scolded in mock anger. "I am the one, who asks the questions."

"But, Master, I must question you. When I think you're going to be upset with me, you are happy. When I think you will rejoice with me, it brings you pain. I must question you about these things. I do not understand how they can be."

"Do you remember yesterday?" he asked quizzically.

"Of course," I replied, "I will never forget yesterday."

"This morning you tried to convince me that you didn't need to experience today, because of yesterday. Isn't that right?"

I nodded my agreement, as I lowered my head. Once again the awful foolishness of childhood rushed at me, and I was ashamed. Whatever illusion the day produced, I was still what I was at the beginning of the day, to assume more could only further prove my ignorance.

"Master," I vowed, "I will never forget one minute of my time with you. It is, somehow, being chiseled into the fiber of a part of my heart, a part I never knew existed."

"Be that as it may," he continued, moving his hands in a way that discounted my compliment and brushed it out of the way. "You were speaking as though you have reached some sort of an end. That, is the reason I said you were like me. We are so foolish. You were looking for an end, an end to childhood. Can you see the irony here? Can you see the core of my foolishness to this very day?"

I was tempted to nod agreement, but I knew that I would only be guessing. I was never sure where the Master was going. "I am not sure I follow you." I said weakly.

"What was it that happened to you today? Was it an end or a beginning?"

"It was a beginning," I flushed, "a point to mark my life from."

"But, you reported it to me as though it were an end. Now you have arrived at some proper way to think and act. Do you see?" he asked earnestly.

"It's true," I retorted, "and I will try to think that way for the rest of my life, regardless of what you tell me." My defiance surprised me.

"I am not trying to say that you did anything wrong," he explained, "only that there is more. You only told me what you thought and what you felt. You could not tell me anything that happened."

"I was so astounded at what was happening to me. I could not notice anything else, at least nothing of importance. I think I was aware of everything out there today. I thought I was seeing everything. That was why I became so excited."

"Well," he laughed, "tomorrow you will see about that. Or will you argue with me again, about walking alone?"

"No Master, I will do as you say." I said, but I wondered what new thing could possibly be out there that could rival the last few days.

"Master, are you telling me for certain there will be

a something new to see tomorrow?" I ask incredulously. "I have learned so much, how could there be more?"

"Still the questions, how many times must I tell you?" he laughed. "I ask the questions. Remember? Besides, there will be only one way for you to find out, regardless of what I say." As he talked, a knowing smile spread across his face.

"Master," I said, now feeling very comfortable about being a child again. "I do not think my brain can hold more. Another day may burst me."

"Another day could be your last," he deadpanned, "whether we put more in you, or not."

It was not a comfortable place to stop our conversation, but the Master announced it by laboring to rise. I did not notice the lengthening shadows until he stood. Once again, time had been racing along while I wasn't watching. Another day was gone. How many more days, like this, would I know in my life? How could something so full be so short? It mystified me.

CHAPTER 16

We walked directly to the road in the morning. I tried to ask tricky questions, to get some idea what the Master expected me to get out of the day, but he insisted upon babbling along on any number of subjects.

What were the attributes of a truly good worker, of a good manager? Did I think there were animals in nature who ran the affairs of other animals like men do of other men?

It did not matter how skillfully I chose my words. He pursued only the answers to his questions. It was comforting and disquieting at once. I could not tell if he was skillfully avoiding me or seeking answers to his questions.

Our parting contained none of the ceremony of the other days. There was no dialog. "I will see you under the tree." he said. Then, he turned like an old soldier, bent over, but still resolute.

My first thought was to recreate the day before. As I walked, I consciously alerted my hearing to reach out. I issued my eyes specific orders as to what to look for. My feet assumed a rhythm that would allow me to move as quickly as possible, while attending to my safety.

The task at hand was walking. I approached it as a task.

I was thinking about something else when I passed my first day's landmark of terror. I realized that I'd passed it after it was out of sight behind me.

How different a few days can make things. Four days before this road had been like a nightmare to me. Today, that experience was a memory etched in the past. The same road now served as subject matter for a report I did not know how to make.

What could I possibly tell the Master? Would he be happy or upset because I passed through the crisis spot without bothering to give it a thought?

A bird fluttered by straining slightly as it flew. A small lizard of some sort hung out of its mouth. It landed in the fork of a small low hung tree and surveyed the area. Then it began to tear its prey apart, and seemed to drop the pieces into a hole in the trunk of the tree.

I drew closer carefully, and heard the squeaking of tiny mouths. A new generation of predator was being raised. Once the feeding was completed and the parent flew away, I moved over to the tree. The stumpy base made it easy to climb high enough to look down into the nest.

I was shocked to see two different birds in the nest. One was brown and tan speckled, obviously like the parent bird. Its coloration was almost identical, but the other chick was quite different. It was almost half again as large and solid dull black in color. I knew that sometimes male and female birds look very different, so it seemed logical to assume that this larger chick was the male of the species. I made some mental notes and resolved to look up this species of birds in my reference book at home; however many species of Indian birds were not included, so I knew my best source would be the Master.

Further down the road, I stopped at one of the bushes that served as the farm and battleground for the ants and beetles. This bush had two beetles attacking, and the ants were getting no rest at all. The chaos and pitch of the battle amazed me even more when I considered that I could be totally unaware of the drama if I moved a few steps away.

"How much more was there to see?" I wondered and walked on.

I heard a rodent or small animal flush and rustle through some of the thick grasses on the edge of the road. The soft rustle of the escape erupted into a rolling thrash. I never saw anything, but I knew what happened. My ears told me that this poor animal had rushed headlong into a hunting snake. The question rose in my mind as to whether it was a cobra or not, but prudence seemed to dictate that certain information was not always needed. This was certainly one of those times, so I went on.

Little things kept catching my attention. As I investigated them, other events became apparent to me. As I stood still investigating one drama, another would capture my attention. As I investigated that, other things would show themselves. As I stood still observing, activity burst out all around me, activity that I had never seen before.

A hypothesis formed in my mind. Every time I stopped to investigate something, I began to see other things; therefore, if I stop anywhere, and look long enough, I will see things happen.

It was an easy hypothesis to test. I simply picked a likely spot and froze. I moved only my eyes and head ever so slightly.

It took a minute, perhaps two, and there was a flicker

of movement. A lizard, frozen at my arrival, moved a few blurred steps to get to a more concealed spot. I noticed a flower with several bugs laboring to rob it of its precious bounty. The bugs were oblivious to me and to the fact that they were being used by the plant to reproduce. They had hairy areas on their sides and backs that were covered with yellowish pollen. A spider danced before my eyes. A large fly dangled by a few threads in its web. Each time the spider moved back and forth across the web another strand of silk imprisoned the fly. Each strand further assured the death of the still struggling fly, while it assured the continued life of the spider. When it finished covering one area, the spider strung two quick connections to the web and dropped down to repeat the process on a lower part of the fly. Once the fly was completely helpless and escape was impossible, the spider cut all the connections but one and began turning the now encased fly with its legs. Life could be so easy with eight legs. It spun the fly with two legs, spread its silk with two and hung on the web with the other four.

Movement below me drew my attention to the ground, again. A beetle had been crawling unobserved by me, but not by the lizard. When the lizard leaped to the attack, my first thought was that, at least, I was innocent of the beetles life. He was not fleeing me when death met him. He was just going about business.

The lizard seemed a little proud of itself as it pranced back into the protective depths of the bush, but before he reached the safety of the morass of branches and twigs, another hunter stood before him.

Another lizard was obviously contending for the kill. He grabbed at the beetle and a short scuffle ensued. The battle was over almost before it began. I assumed it was because the lizards were about the same size and the original hunter had a firm grip on the beetle. He could not be intimidated into releasing his grip. Still strutting the tiny hunter paraded into the underbrush with his kill.

I was left wondering what might have happened had the second lizard been a little larger. In my mind, I saw him on top of the smaller one wrenching the beetle out of his helpless mouth.

I wanted to taunt the loser a little, so I reached out toward it. The lizard rushed away from my hand, but it did not go back into the thick growth. Instead, it ran wildly out across the path.

It did not reach the other side. Another hunter had obviously been watching the whole drama. A bird, perhaps the same bird I watched feed its young swooped down with fluttering wings and carried the lizard off into the air.

This was one death I had participated in. My actions forced the lizard away from the safety of the bush and into the open. His demise was part of my presence.

So it continued, all along the Flood Road. Each time I tested my theory a whole new cast of characters in the drama of life showed themselves to me. They were there every time I stopped long enough to allow them to show themselves.

I became more aware of the respect nature has for man. Man is like a king in nature. Everything stops for him. Well, maybe not the tiger. I realized then why tigers must hunt from the shadows. Everything stops for them, too. The cobra must hunt slowly for the same reason. It was so obvious to me, now.

I remembered the Master's conviction that there was a purpose or reason for everything. Nothing happens by accident. Everything has its place. The smaller and weaker you are, the more important it is for you to watch where you're going. When you are small enough like the ants, you just go about your business. You are so small that your life or death doesn't matter. The children will still be cared for.

Everything fit together for me on that walk. It did not end when I reached the end of the Flood Road. It continued all the way back to town. As I reached the first buildings I realized it was late in the afternoon. My day disappeared into the Master's world without him.

CHAPTER 17

I still had to report to the Master, so I raced directly to the tree.

"Good, I'm glad you're here." he said. "We were just discussing whether I needed to come looking for you or go eat. Now we can just eat, and then you can tell me of your day."

They should have been eating the last of the chickens I provided for this meal. I made a mental note to bring more chickens and a bag of rice in the morning, and tried to excuse myself.

"But, we have not had a chance to talk." smiled the Master. "Eat with us. I will send one of the boys to tell Silke and Faude that you will be late. They will not worry."

"Yes, but they wait each night for me." I protested.

"They know that I have been waiting to meet you for twelve years." the Master said with a smile that told me there was much more involved in all this than I knew. "They worked for your grandfather, too. They know me. It will be fine."

I think he sensed my uneasiness with the other people. I was not used to being around poor people.

"It would be good for you to stay." he said, almost in

a whisper. "There is something for you to learn here as well."

His words carried with them the authority of my teacher and I did not argue anymore.

They were good people. I think my presence bothered them a little, too.

I was really surprised at how good the broth was. I was hungry, for sure, after a day in the bush, but the broth seemed far better than it could possibly be. There were few vegetables, and while rice was obviously the main ingredient; it was used sparingly, at least according to what I was used to. Still, I marveled at each sip. Poor people were not that poor if what they ate tasted like this. Perhaps, that was why they only used one chicken. It was all that they needed. I was glad I could honestly thank the woman so profusely for the broth she made. I think she enjoyed the compliment, as well. Bowing to them all, I gave my thanks. The Master led me back to his house for my report.

"I did not see everything, but I tried." I began.

"Surely something happened differently." he questioned. "You took so much longer today."

"That is why I was so late." I explained. "I began to notice things I never noticed before. Once it started, I couldn't stop it. One discovery always led me to another."

The Master leaned backwards, slowly. His eyes were closed and a smile of satisfaction spread across his face. He was not smiling at me, but appeared to be saying the thanks of an answered prayer.

"Now I can die in peace." he said. He breathed out heavily as though a burden had been removed from him. His eyes twinkled when he brought his gaze back to me. "The promise I gave your grandfather has been kept. In a few days you have learned all the lessons of my lifetime. Now, if you pursue them, you will spend the rest of your lifetime learning them, again and again."

"Master, I had a wonderful day!" I exclaimed. "You have almost made it sound like a prison sentence. I do not understand what you are saying. You said, I have learned all the lessons you have spent a lifetime learning, and in the same breath you say I will have to learn them over and over, if I pursue them. When a student learns a lesson, he goes on to the next lesson. Why would I choose to condemn myself to such repetition?"

"Your thinking may be correct in your geometry and economics," he said happily, "but it has not been my experience in life. I have been compelled to learn the same lessons over and over. Such is the state of mankind. Such is the state of our intellect."

"How can you speak such terrible words with such a happy face?" I broke in, confused and helpless again. "You always confuse me. Bad things become good and good things become bad."

"That is almost it, exactly." the Master rejoiced. "But, do not stop with that thought. Consider for a moment how great and how awesome the One you are studying must be, forever different, always new and in each and every instance the same."

He was dancing again, waving his arms from side to side and stamping his frail feet on the ground floor. He continued in a circle until he came back to me. He bent down and got very close to me.

"Do you remember?" he asked. "You and I are but helpless children trying to understand something so far above us, that we are lost in it. We are like two year old children. We have a Father, who is at work all around us, but we cannot begin to comprehend all that He does or all the ways that He cares for us. We simply learn again and again that everything is under control and that He loves us.

What a wonderful journey it will be for you. What a wonderful seeking. Can there be a higher thing to strive for? Can there be a better thing to see again and again?"

"Master. Wait. You are going to fast for me." I pleaded, "Slow down."

"I am not telling you anything new." he smiled. "I see the need for truth in your eyes.

Now tell me of your day, and we shall see if what I have said becomes any plainer to you."

I started immediately with the odd birds in the nest. As soon as I began describing them to him, the Master began rocking back and forth approvingly.

"Yes. Yes." he mused picturing them in his eyes. "The cowchasers and the robber birds, I have watched and wondered about them for years. It is another of the unanswered mysteries I will probably die with. They used to threaten me, the mysteries, not the birds. I hated the thought of dying in ignorance, but I have so many questions. I have resolved myself." The Master's eyes sparkled and his smile radiated a satisfaction that did not fit his hopeless words.

"The whole thing is a mystery to me." he began. "At first, I thought they were male and female, who had drastically different life styles and appearances, but there were always two cowchasers feeding the babies. I never saw one robber bird bring food to the nest. It became apparent to me that the two cowchasers must be male and female. That is the way things are done with birds. Both parents work full-time feeding the chicks. How the robber birds came to give up their parenting roles is beyond me. I do not think it is a matter of laziness, though, for I have seen them work most industriously to steal a meal from another bird, harder, in fact, than if they worked for it themselves.

It has always been the same. Whenever I have seen a new cowchasers nest, I find one egg in it. The first egg is always the spotted brown egg. Then a few days later, I find the second egg. It is always the rounder solid brown one. Two weeks later the solid brown egg always hatches three or four days ahead of the speckled one. It is like clockwork.

I know the speckled egg is laid at least four days ahead of the brown one, but the brown one always hatches first. The brown egg always becomes the robber bird.

They are vibrant chicks, full of life. From the moment they are born, they seem to be able to see and move very well. The cowchaser chicks, on the other hand, are born quite helpless. They are barely able to lift their head at birth. It takes a week before the cowchaser can begin to compete for food. The poor cowchaser parents must satisfy the robber bird chick before their own can get any food at all."

I was mystified. My small mystery became a great one. "What could it be Master? What is your hypothesis?"

"So, you are going to make me into a scientist, are you?" he laughed. "Well, I do have a theory, but it still has a hook, a question at the end of it."

"What is it, Master?" I asked. "Isn't that what you just told me? I am embarking on a never ending journey."

"And you," he squealed in joyful irritation, "are trying to play the teacher again."

He paused, as he gathered his thoughts.

"To me," he began, "they must be two different birds. The cowchasers are hardworking, industrious birds. Robber birds are the same sneaking thieves they are known for. The robber bird sneaks into the cowchasers nest and lays its egg, and then lets the cowchasers rear its baby."

"How can that be, Master?" I asked, incredulous. "How can a thing like instinct tell one kind of bird to lay its egg in another's nest? Where could it have begun? How could it have been done the first time?"

"You are asking the questions again." he scolded. "Besides that! You ask questions that I ask, and cannot answer." There was satisfaction in his voice.

"I only know this," he said, now very serious and lost in the mystery of many years. "I have seen cowchaser nests that never got a second egg, and I never saw one of those chicks live to leave the nest, never, not one. Whenever the second egg appears, the cowchaser baby lives to fly away. So I have concluded that, somehow the presence of the robber bird chick guarantees the survival of the cowchasers."

"So," I interrupted, "your hypothesis is that somehow, the presence of the robber bird is tied to survival of the cowchaser chick?"

"Exactly." he said. "I knew you were that way. Tomorrow we must go to the nest and see it."

"Master," I said, "if we go to the nest tomorrow, we must walk the road together."

"There is no longer any need for you to go alone." he said simply. "We should go together so we can see more."

A sensation seeped into my soul. It was satisfaction. It was also a sense of beginning. It was a step into manhood that I would share with a man nearly at the end of his walk through life. There was no place on earth I would rather be.

I shook my head. "Master," I confessed, "I was sure that you would not be happy with my report. It seemed to me that you were never happy about the things I thought should make you happy."

He smiled. "Suppose, I said that I believe we were never to be too happy or too comfortable with anything." He was toying with me again. "Suppose, I felt an obligation not to be satisfied. Suppose, I consider that my main purpose as your teacher is to teach you dissatisfaction."

"You are playing with me again Master." I said. "What do you know, that you want me to know?"

"And, you are not supposed to ask the questions." he squealed in delight. "It is simple," he continued, "I want you to be happy and fulfilled, and never satisfied. I want to take any idea of self-satisfaction away from you."

"I thought self-awareness and self-satisfaction were the highest form of mental and spiritual development." I said, summarizing the whole of my religious training.

"I understand what you are saying." he continued. "I do not contend with those theories. I only argue with making that the highest goal." He stopped talking and looked away, as if considering whether to go on or not.

"Master, what can be greater than oneness with the universe? I've never understood that concept. I can see it now, because you took me into the tall grasses. The idea is very comforting to me, now."

"What if there is something higher than the universe?"

At first I thought he was making a joke, but his eyes showed me he was quite serious.

"What if the universe is only a mural painted by a hand so awesome that the whole of creation is only a few brushstrokes?" Tears welled up in his eyes and he looked off through the open door to hold them in.

"I am a wicked wretch." he announced with conviction. "I deserve only to die and rot. How can I speak these things with you? I must be getting senile. I've never allowed one of my students to pry these out of me."

"Master!" I pleaded, "You have done nothing wrong to me, only good things, things that have changed the kind of man I will be for the better."

"It may seem that way to you," he said sadly, "but I have a fear. I have come to consider that the painter watches his masterpiece, and that there will be a day of accountability for every person.

My observations have led me to conclude that man is different from the other creatures. He alone is equipped to stand back and evaluate the painting, to ponder the character of the painter."

"But, what crime is there in your words?" I argued. "You have said nothing to me that disrespects the painter."

"And, you do not understand the responsibility of the teacher." he responded in a nearly despondent voice. "It does not matter so much if I live my life unawares, that is bad enough, mind you. But, if I influence others, you, and I do so wrongly, if I lead you into empty things, I am sure that it will be brought back to me. It is one thing to think and live, but it is another to think and teach.

It is easy to become intoxicated with teaching. I have seen it in myself and in others. It is a frightening thing, especially when teaching is all that your soul hopes for, when it is the highest thing you could aspire to in your life. There is an obligation.

What if I make you unproductive, with my teaching?"

He was waiting for an answer.

"Master," I cried, "a few days ago I was a protected child. I lived in a world where the study of a subject could be measured by appropriate responses or the number of pages read. But now, I have walked the road alone, the only option before me was to see and live. You brought me to that place in days, and I shall never be the same again. Whereever I go and whatever I do, I will strive to see all that I can. You are responsible for that. If that is a sin, perhaps you should be proud to stand in your sin."

"That appears to be true," he said, holding me by the shoulders. "My problem is that I have seen so many things that appeared to be true. They feel good and look good. They are always so reasonable, and then in time, I find my error. I think it is the main weakness of mankind. We easily accept what appears to be true. I fight against it constantly, for I see the roots of the weakness ever in me.

Animals do not seem to be inclined in this way. They live and they die. They perform the tasks they were designed for."

"Master," I interrupted, "I cannot comprehend a god so cruel, so as to hold you accountable in your earnestness."

"Cruel," he pondered the word. "awesome, all-powerful, all-knowing, what do those words mean?" He flicked his hand to the side, as if disdainful of the thought. "A great ruler is called cruel by those he rules against and awesome by those he favors.

I only know my place. I can see that clearly. I am so far below that I can only expect to be ruled against. I only see my ignorance."

"What if that is the proper conclusion?" I asked, lost in an idea I'd never considered. "Suppose that is the only right observation to make?"

His eyes gleamed at me.

"It seems too high a thing to hope for," he smiled,

"but that is my conclusion, too. I can only be true to what I see to be true. It is the only concept I have, to hope in."

"Master, I would never think or act in a way just because you told me to do so."

"Teachers have a power," he said, "you do not have to give them the authority. As soon as you allow them to speak, you give them power over you. It doesn't matter whether you know it or not.

We have much to do tomorrow. You should go home, now."

"But I have only begun my report." I responded.

"There will be time in the morning." he assured me, and he rose to walk me out the door, effectively ending any further discussion on the matter.

This was a day when the shadows of a full moon were my companions home.

CHAPTER 18

Silke and Faude had everything ready for me when I arrived. They were ready to feed me just in case I was not full, but I declined.

I was never a big eater, so Silke did not sound too concerned when she remarked how little I was eating. She was right. I was eating only two meals a day and gave little thought to food. Hunger arrived only after my day with the Master was completed.

It made me reconsider his words about the authority of a teacher. My mind was giving him so much of my attention that it was forgetting about food. Could it be that he was right? What if he was leading me into areas and attitudes about the gods, which would be the ruin of me? I'd heard about such things in barbaric cultures.

It perplexed me for a few moments. I considered how little I really knew about anything in life. That helplessness was what finally comforted me. I remembered the Master's exhortation. "Never, forget that you are a helpless child."

Over the years, I have enjoyed the experience several times. Whenever I became totally immersed in a project, I forget to eat. It was to become a sign to me, both of caution and inspiration.

Silke and Faude were both beaming. Once they had

assured themselves that I was not going to seat myself at the table, Silke stepped forward. "We have wonderful news." she announced, "A steamship arrived today from upriver. Your father sent a message that he was returning early from his trip. He will return on the next boat, either tomorrow or the day after."

The thought thrilled me, now we would have something to share, both of us walked the road alone. My mind conjured up visions of Father. His eyes were lit with images of his own battle with fear and the unknown, and the journeys of his youth with the Master. His words flowed easily as he remembered his boyhood with me.

I began to prepare my presentation for him. I would need to be clear and concise. Father was used to that. He demanded it from his employees.

I often heard him say the same thing, "I do not care why it happened, for now. I need to know what happened and what you have done to fix the problem. We will have plenty of time to assure that the problem will not return, after it is not a problem any more."

I always liked it when he became upset like that. After the foreman or supervisor left, Father would turn to me. "You must always keep your head clear." he would say. "Deal with the moment, later you will have time to go back over it in your mind. Get the information you need to make good decisions. Train your workers and your sons to do the same."

Of course! It was one of his lessons from the road. I was sure of it.

There would be so much for us to talk about. Finally, I began to feel an understanding for him. I remembered the Master's words. "If he could not measure something, hold it, or count it, it was of no use to him, even as a child." I began to see how he became the man he had become, not just my father.

It was not the death of my mother that drove us apart. He could not measure that pain. So he did what he could, he worked. You can measure work. I saw that I unconsciously thought that he blamed me for her death.

I cried again, for her.

The softness of my mother returned to me. The love in her eyes touched me again. She was the one who told me what a wonderful man my father was. I was never able to see it before, but perhaps now, I was beginning to.

I was in a dilemma. How could I report concisely? Each day, each lesson was like a book in itself.

I laughed when I considered the first day. I was going to educate this old man. My role in life would be dealing with simple, uneducated people. What foolishness it was, what profound ignorance. My father had skillfully scheduled my experience with this old man to prepare me for my higher education in Calcutta.

How could I report about the fear, the cold, killing, strangulating fear? How did the Master present it to my father? Oh, the wonder of it! Now we had a common ground, a place that both of us knew. I could not wait to hear my father tell me of his experiences. He was always very clear and concise, so I would understand easily.

Then the question arose. Which was the greatest lesson? Perhaps, I should focus on just one day. I could not evaluate my lessons that way. Each day had its place like steps on a stairs. One could not be singled out from the rest as more valuable than the others. There was a progression that necessitated both the previous and the next step.

It was impossible. Finally, I purposed to discuss it with the Master in the morning.

Sleep did not come easily that night.

CHAPTER 19

Silke and Faude were very excited the next morning. They heard a steamship would be in, down river, that afternoon. I wasn't as affected, schedules on the river were subject to the whims of the river. Boats were sometimes two and three days late. I was hoping for more time to prepare for Father.

I ate my morning meal as quickly as possible, filling myself to the brim. It would likely be a long day. I wondered what and how much the Master ate for his morning meal.

He was waiting for me under the tree. He reacted happily when I told him Father might return that day.

"I'm sure he will come today." he said. "He was always punctual, punctual to a fault." I could see that he was remembering my father as a child in his eyes. He was obviously looking at something that wasn't under the tree with us.

"Master," I said, "I had trouble going to sleep last night. I tried to prepare myself for my report to Father. When I think about my lessons, I am overwhelmed. Each lesson is like a story in itself. I know that Father does not like long stories."

"Indeed," he giggled, "that is your father. Tell me

what happened and do not waste any words, about it.' Your father was so different from your grandfather. Do not worry. It is just the way he is."

"I know, but . . . ," I hesitated.

"What is wrong?" he asked, now more concerned.

"I was hoping . ." I said, lowering my head, "I was hoping that my experiences on the road would get my father to tell me his stories. Now we have something we share. We both sat under your teaching. Now, I know why he is a wise man, it is because of you and your teaching."

The Master's laugh protested. "If he is a wise man, it is not because of me. It is because he sought after and recognized the truth. That is what makes any person wise. What do you think?"

How I wished the Master had been my grandfather. I could have sat on his lap and leaned my head into his chest to hear the high laughter through his flesh. His laughter was, at once, silly and comforting. I was a boy, trying to be a man, wanting to be a child, with him.

"I think," he continued, "that wisdom is a process. It is not a state of mind people attain. Could it be that people cannot become wise? They can only be wise. Every man is wise when he seeks the truth, without restriction. Can you see now why you had to walk the road alone? I put you in a place that would force you to see with every part of your mind and being."

"I only know, that I am glad that I did. I will be forever grateful that you insisted. But, how will that help me report properly to my father?"

"Perhaps, you will not have to." he mused.

"Oh, Master, it has always been that way, even before Mother died. When Father came home from a trip, I would go into his study and report everything I was learning in school. Whenever I got off-track, he would stop me and bring me back to the exact subject at hand."

"That is not what I meant." the Master stopped me. "Perhaps the experience you both share will be evident to him. You may not need to report it."

The thought exhilarated me. I had changed. If I really was different, it was reasonable that Father would see that change on me, when I went in to him. Perhaps that would be enough.

"I have been with the Master every day since you left." I would say. "I have walked the road alone." What more would I have to say? His own experience with the Master should tell him of my lessons.

Besides another subject demanded attention.

"Master," I queried, "I know that what you say is true. I see that a man can only be wise, but it makes me wonder if a healthy cow is wise."

"Are you trying to become the questioner, again?" he teased, still the question intrigued him. "Whatever do you mean?" he asked a little bewildered.

"You said a man is wise when he acts wisely and seeks the truth." I replied.

"Yes, and I believe that it is the only way we puny creatures can reach higher things." he answered back.

This time, I was sure I was the one who saw a truth worth seeing.

"Well, according to your definition, the only requirement of a healthy cow would be one who eats. If the cow eats, the eating will have its effect and the cow will be healthy." I moved my hands to gesture how simple the conclusion must be.

"I still cannot see your point." he said thoughtfully.

That moment was another special point in my life. The Master was actually following me. He wanted to know what I thought. To him, I was not a ridiculous child.

"Master," I explained, "if a cow is fed poor food it will not matter how much it eats. It will always be less than it could be, but if the cow is fed good rich food, it will be healthier, even if it eats less."

He was laughing now. "You win." he laughed, "I concede your point. You will be a shrewd negotiator for your father."

"Master," I insisted, "you must let me say this. The lessons you taught me were good food. Yes, I was a willing learner, but I was just like a cow willing to eat whatever it was fed. You have fed me rich lessons. I only ate them. You taught my father." I named off the men Faude told me about. "You taught all of them; therefore, you must accept credit, at least some credit for them. We must say that they are being wise in their decisions today, partly because of being fed the lessons you taught them."

He did not protest. He simply nodded and looked down humbly.

"It was always my goal for them all." he confessed. "Understand me when I say that I cannot blindly be satisfied for them, any more than I can be for me. My satisfaction does not come from looking back at them. I am compelled to seek satisfaction in the day before me."

"Master, I do not think I understand." I said.

"Enough is never enough." he explained without emotion. "Once you have come to that conclusion, where can you go?

A man who burns after riches will never have enough. He will forever strive to reach the high point before him, only to find another high point on the horizon beyond him.

Wisdom is the same, really. Truth is the same. They are like a treasure that shines as brilliantly as a necklace of gold and emeralds."

He was gazing now, off into an unseen horizon, filled with images I could only imagine.

"It cannot be you." he said suddenly. "I am senile. I am getting ready to die. Every conversation brings us to the same place." His voice was resolute and empty.

"My heresy stands before me, again. What shall I do?" he asked, but the question was not directed at me.

"Perhaps, you should . ." I stopped. "Perhaps, you are supposed to tell me your heresy." I gulped.

He was silent for a few moments. His head was bowed down. Finally, he turned to me. "Perhaps, you are right." he said simply.

"We are such a lucky people," he began. "We have so many deities to aid us. When I was a boy, I tried so hard to measure the length and breadth of them all.

One night, I was sitting on the great river, alone. The moon was low in the sky and beautiful. Its reflection filled the river and shimmered in another, different beauty. Both of the moons were beautiful. One was the real moon and one was the reflection. . . ."He hesitated. "And then, I heard a voice. It was One Being. It was the Painter. 'Everything that is before you is a reflection of Me.' He said. 'I have set Myself in all My painting in hopes that I would be seen. I desire to show Myself.'"

The Master sighed. "I am convinced," he continued, "that everything that is before us is the reflection of one God. A God so great and awesome that we have been forced to give Him many names and personalities. It is only because our understanding is so limited. So there you have it. There is only one God!" he said with finality. "That God is truth and love. His name might as well be Truth and Love. Here in this life we have hatred and untruth, but none of that exists in Him. I know that, because I have heard his voice. We must give names to the evil gods, when we are confronted by evil. I am convinced that if there is something else that appears to man to be a god, it will still bend to the knee before that One that I heard. They all bend down to the Painter."

"Master," I said, "it all sounds so wonderful. Why do you sound so unhappy?"

"We started all this with my dissatisfaction, remember?" he said. "I have searched and searched, but I do not have a name to call out. What is worse, the more I learn about this Painter, the more I am confronted by the impossibility of my search. That God is so awesome, so perfect and high, that I do not have any hope of being heard.

Soon, I will die, and I will go out saying, 'I do not know what name to call.' It is all so hopeless.

How can I inflict such a desperate teaching on you? It is unthinkable that I might put such uncertainty upon you, into your young life."

"Master, I will not follow you down that road unless I am led there. Since my mother died, I have not found comfort in any of the gods."

"Right now, comfort is not my concern," he shot back testily, "only grievous error."

"To be honest with you," I blurted, "I do not think I can accept your conclusion."

He did not say anything, waiting for me to continue.

"We have discussed how the spiritual is mirrored in the physical." I began. "It seems most reasonable to me to conclude that the gods are people on a spiritual plane. They have status and levels of interest. They have different roles and functions just as we do. Yes, it would even be right that they have different personalities and inclinations toward good and evil."

"I agree," he said, "yours is the most reasonable perspective." With that he began the slightly labored process of rising.

"Master, where are you going?" I asked, startled at the abruptness of his surrender.

"What more is there to say?" he shrugged, with a hint of relief. "Your version is definitely the most reasonable. I concede; besides, if we walk, we can still talk and we can allow the gods ample opportunity to walk with us."

At first, I thought he was making fun of me, but the flow of conversation between us convinced me that he was trying his utmost to sound as though my argument had carried the day.

CHAPTER 20

The tree had become quite crowded as merchants and street peddlers set themselves up in the shade of the tree. We were beginning our walk much later than usual.

"Master?" I queried.

"Why do I sense another question coming?" he laughed.

"I'm sorry," I confessed, "but I cannot allow our discussion of the gods to end like this. I would prefer to talk about my father, to ready myself in case he returns tonight."

"Your choice of words about your father concern me." he said, carefully. "Why don't we talk about him now. Later, when we are on the road, we can talk more of my folly."

"What do you mean, my choice of words?" I asked.

"What do you mean, when you say, 'I must report to my father?" he wondered. "How does that event take place?"

"Usually, we know when father will return. He sends notice on a boat a day or two ahead, but we never know what time he will come home. Often, he attends to matters in the warehouses, first. My report will be given with the evening meal, unless I have already eaten. If I have eaten, Father will eat in his study. I will go to him there.

A couple of times I've been asleep when he returned. If it's not too late Faude will wake me up and send me to him.

It is always the same report. The questions are always the same.

'Tell me what you've learned in school.' he will say.

I try to impress him with volume and variety. He stops me and asks how this or that will affect my ability to evaluate people or information."

"Yes, yes," smiled the Master, "I can easily see him sitting there.

Tell me, does he ask if you have had fun learning, if you have enjoyed your lessons?"

My head must have dropped like a lead weight.

"No Master, that is why I was hopeful about this report. My fondest hope is that tonight he will talk to me. Just talk. You know?

You say that I ask all the questions. Perhaps, it is from the build up. Somehow, I never get to ask him questions. It is I who report.

That was why I could not sleep last night. I imagined my father telling me the stories of his youth, with you."

"I'm afraid that is not one of his strong points." the Master said softly.

"Now that I have been with you, I see that better." I replied. I knew it was true, but I could still hope.

"Perhaps something will happen," he continued. "Perhaps, I will get to speak to him again and I can broach the subject."

I kept silent. I did not understand before, but now I recognized that the comments I'd heard my father make about the Master were not misinterpretations on my part. My father really did consider the Master to be irrelevant, and unuseful in a modern age. I knew the odds were very slim that Father would take the time to see him.

"Thank you." I said. I knew only that I was very, very glad that Father had given me to the Master. I wished he had done it years before.

We were nearing the Flood Road. We had already investigated half a dozen minor wonders.

The Master congratulated me on my technique of observation. We stopped at likely spots and waited to see what was really there.

"Do you think that this technique could have any application in the world of men and business?" he asked.

"I never thought about it that way," I said, "but I suppose it must be so."

"I think it does." he continued. "So often I found that I and others were moving around trying to stay on top of things. No matter what we did, it seemed that something was always out of place somewhere else. It was only after I stopped for a little bit just to watch, that I was better able to determine what really needed to be done.

I saw evidence of the same truth as a teacher. I became frustrated with some of the children. They were not all as open and receptive as you are. Some of them were rebellious."

The thought that a child might be disrespectful to the Master amazed me. On the whole, children were very respectful in school. Occasionally, some did talk back to our teachers in the private school.

He continued, "Some seemed slow to me. I became irritated when they did not or could not see the value of my lessons. Remember, I used to teach reading and counting, too.

I found that I could achieve more with the difficult students when I stopped trying to teach and just watched them. Once I saw more about them, what they were interested in and what they were good at, I was better able to construct my lessons so they would learn.

The rebellious ones were just like fish." he laughed, "I had to learn what made them bite." He laughed more, as he remembered.

I longed to call his blood into my veins.

We stopped and walked over to a tree that had fallen into the river. A large yellow sandbar rose out of the murky darkness on either side and glistened like an amber gem, just below the surface.

"Have you watched fish much?" he asked. "They are incredible. Life and death in the water is a matter of an arm's length, no more."

"We stood over the seemingly barren sandbar for several moments, waiting. A small discoloration flickered and moved a couple of body lengths. Then, as if by magic, twenty or thirty small fish appeared. They were suspended motionless at our approach. They only became visible when they began to move again.

The surface of the water at our feet began to dimple. First tens, then hundreds, and then thousands of tiny fish began to crowd the surface at the shoreline.

"They must be careful," whispered the Master, "the fish birds are attracted to movement. Have you ever watched any of the shoremasters fish? They stand on those long legs and move like a cat stalking a mouse. They must look like a stick, or they will never eat. The fish do not know the difference between us and a shoremaster, so they freeze for us, too. The problem is that sooner or later somebody has to move, so it's a waiting game. Life goes on, but death comes for some."

"Master," I whispered, "do you see one god here?"

"You should not make fun of a foolish old man." he whispered back. "I have conceded your point. Good manners demand the matter be dropped there."

"I think you only conceded the point to me to free yourself of any obligation to explain yourself further." I said. "My words were honest."

"Your grandfather would have challenged me like that." the Master said with satisfaction and sorrow. "Why do you demand my answers to questions I have not been able to answer for myself? These are my sorrows. Why do you ask that I share them with you?"

"Master, you told me we were helpless children. You told me never to forget that. I do not ask you to torment you, but only to find a truth for myself. You said we could talk more about the idea of there being only one god when we were on the road. This should be close enough."

"The other way is so much more comfortable for me." he sighed.

"It is also more comfortable for me to refuse any thought that I might forever be a helpless child." I countered. "What comfort would you give me in that, except that your observations have convinced you that it was true."

"Once again, you win." he laughed. "I have to be senile. I used to be able to stay ahead of my students, a little. Either that, or you are your grandfather. He used to challenge me unmercifully."

"I said I believed there was only one god, because He told me so. There, does that satisfy you? Did you hear me say it? I didn't say just one main god. I didn't say They said or It said, I said, He said. God is a being, like you and I. He is the Father, not a father or like a father. He is the Father. I could tell it in His voice. Are you still with me?" he demanded.

I shook my head to confirm that I was, but I wondered why such precision of wordage was needed.

His voice, which was loud and animated, became distant and solemn.

"I did not hear it, but I understood it in my hearing."

"This is so hopeless for me," he protested shaking his head. "I do not understand these things for myself."

"Please, Master. Try." I pleaded.

The Master looked at me and breathed deeply.

"He said, 'All of this is here for you. All that is before you is a representation of Me. Study them and you study Me.'

Well, I did study and I have seen wonderful things. It is all so personal. I heard it said once, that artists paint themselves into every picture. An expert can name the artist by their style. What a beautiful thought.

He is the Father-Creator. He is the Mother-Nourisher. He is the Warrior-Protector. He is the King-Sovereign. He is the Builder-Worker. He is the Farmer-Tender. He is the Painter-Artist.

"Master, I think I am following you," I said, "but, forgive me. I cannot help but argue that you speak only of the roles of man."

"Really," he sniffed, now fully recovered, "and what of the spider's web? Is the spider not both a builder and an artist? Look at the ants you helped me study. They are every bit the farmer. The tiger and cobra are both kings of their empires. Still, they must respect the authority of other kings. Perhaps, you could look at them like farmers, too."

"I just lost you." I interrupted.

"When I was younger, I lived to follow the tiger. I came to know them by their tracks and habits. If a tiger ate deer, he ate the young, the old, and the sick. If the tiger ate pigs, he ate the young, the old, and the sick. The tiger killed what was easiest to kill. When he did that, he acted like a farmer culling his flock."

Just as I was beginning to understand, I noticed the Master was losing the joy of his vision.

"What's wrong Master?" I asked. "I can see your point now. It is an honest vision. I would not have seen it so easily, except for the ants. They are farmers. Indeed, it is the only way they can be classified."

My concession did not restore him. He stood silently staring into the water. Our animated discussion caused the river to appear lifeless again. The activity was only just beginning to swell back up into our vision.

"He has a name." the Master said sadly. "He has a name, and I do not know it."

"Must that be so important?" I asked trying to minimize what seemed only a small point, considering all the titles we just named.

"I guess it is an old man's fallacy." he whispered with a sort of resolute helplessness. "God is such a distant name, like Your Majesty. Have you ever noticed that the better people know each other the less formally they address each other?

Take your grandfather for instance, We were worlds apart in status and caste. As we became close through the years, I came to call him Wild Eyes. I would never call him by that name at the warehouses, but when we were alone, talking . ."

"Whatever did you mean?" I asked. "I thought you loved and respected my grandfather too much to speak to him so disrespectfully."

The Master laughed a joyous laugh and said, "And

you did not know your grandfather. Whenever he became excited with an idea or a thought, his eyes would flair with emotion. It was beautiful to see, that was part of what made him so special to me. When he held an idea in his mind, his eyes held the idea before him. So, you see, it was an intimacy that we shared."

"Did he have a name for you?" I asked, knowing there must be one.

"He called me Teacher." the Master smiled, remembering. "He began a month after I went to work for him." The Master's eyes filled with the memories of another life.

"In the beginning, he meant it a little sarcastically. Some of the other workers complained that I was trying to take over and run the warehouses, but your grandfather was a fair man. When he came to talk to me about it, I attempted to explain myself. I never tried to boss anyone around. I just studied everything. If the results of my study suggested a better way to do a job, I shared it with my coworkers.

Your grandfather, being an astute businessman, appreciated that an employee was trying to find ways to do tasks better, more efficiently. After a few months he promoted me, and made it my job to study how we did things. By that time, he called me Teacher instead of using my real name.

So you see, it was by being a student that I came to be called Teacher.

Do you see what I mean about names now?" he asked.

"I do not desire to call the Great One, God. He came so near to me. If He were a man I would have felt his breath and the heat of His body.

What a fool I am. I cannot explain any of this to myself. How can I possibly find the words for you?"

"Perhaps, you are supposed to try, Master." I interjected, hoping that he would not become discouraged. A sudden flash of thought passed like a wave over me.

"The day I watched you walk back to town from the flood road, I saw that you were going to die, soon. Perhaps you are supposed to tell me of your thoughts." My boldness left me immediately and I dropped my head, supposing that the Master would be angry with my impudence.

"I do not know how I saw it." I continued. "I have never seen anything like that before. When I saw you walking up to the trees and bushes, I saw that you were going to die soon. I was afraid to tell you."

A sweet satisfied chuckle bubbled out of him as he looked up to the sky.

"I have seen it, too." he said. "I have seen it coming like a storm on the horizon. You can watch it come, but it is impossible to tell how fast it is moving, only that it is coming."

"I thought you would be upset with me." I confessed.

"Timing is everything," he whispered emphatically, "and you have chosen well. Perhaps, I should speak as freely as I can to you. It already seems to me that God has sent you to me as a final gift, to make my life complete. My last debt will be paid."

"It is too late anyway." he continued. "I have already told you all that I know, and most of what I think."

CHAPTER 21

He chose that moment to begin walking again. For the first time, I became aware of time on the road. I saw that we were still a long ways from home and the day was well along.

"Master, you never really finished anything." I pleaded.

"It is only because I ran out of words for myself." he laughed. "If more words were there, I would have spoken them just for myself."

"Please, tell me again." I urged.

"There is one God." he said patiently. "He has one voice, one presence. He is a He, but He is both the Mother and the Father of everything that is.

When He came to me in the night, He told me that it was His desire that I know Him. He said, 'I have put Myself in everything that is before you. I have represented Myself in it for you.'

The words I heard were different.

It is not enough to say, the words I heard were from a truthful being. Truth was the substance of the Being.

It is not enough to say His words were filled with love. Love was the Being who spoke them. The words were love.

God is love and God is truth. They are both the same.

They are both Him.

So there you have it. That is everything I know, or at least, everything I think I know.

Everything I have learned in my lifetime of study convinces me, that the words I heard are true. A great Creator has woven a thread of Himself into everything."

"Master, if this great God is only love and truth, and He made everything, why is there so much evil in the world?" I asked.

"I've wondered about that, myself." he chuckled. "Strangely, the more I study evil and hate, the more I must focus on man. I do not see much in nature that you could label as evil. Life and death are natural. In order for something to live, something has to die. It seems to be a law on every level. The tiger must kill to live. The spider must kill to live. The ants must go to war to save their specks. All of them must die to allow the plants to grow. We fertilize with only rotting things, things that have died.

I have seen sights that appear to be cruel. I have seen birds and tigers disable their prey, but there has always been an obvious reason. They had young who were almost grown. It was easy to see that they were teaching their young to hunt and kill. They brought their young living food so they were forced to learn to kill and hunt.

Only man will destroy and kill for pleasure. He makes war with other men. He does despicable things to the women and children of other men. Perhaps there is a reason for the cruelty that is not obvious to me. I have been unable to see one." His eyes returned to me. It was as though he had been talking to himself again and just remembered I was there.

"So my hypothesis is . . . " He emphasized the word for my benefit, "that evil and brutality exist only in man.

I guess it all depends on how you define evil."

"But, Master, that only raises the question of why cruelty should only exist in man." I continued.

"You see," he giggled, "you may already be infected. A question calls for an answer, which begets a question calling for an answer. It has become the pattern of my life. I do not know whether I have spoken a blessing or a curse upon you."

My mind was still examining the question at hand. Why should cvil only exist in and among man. I examined all my experiences from school and with the Master. The books told me of horrible circumstances in the history of man. They told me of the benign goodness of Her Majesty and the English Church. The Monarch of England had been forced to act to combat despicable evil from kings and privateers, conquerors and rebels.

"Master," I said, "It is all so clear to me at this moment, man is the root of all evil, but how can that be possible?"

"I keep telling you that I am the one who asks questions. It is the only thing I am good at."

"Surely, you must have some idea, some hypothesis not yet tested." I countered.

He looked at me quizzically. His eyes smiled with delight and hesitation.

"Somehow, evil is what sets us apart from God. The rest of the creation does not know evil; therefore, it does not know the separation from God. Nature is not forced to perform religious procedures and practices."

"Master there have been more one god people, besides the British. There is a movement to the west. It moved across Africa and Eurasia. I do not know much about it. The teacher in school spoke of it with dread. He said it was very wicked and blood thirsty, but all in the name on one great God."

"I have spoken to some of it's believers already," the Master confided. "They were working on the boats coming upriver from Calcutta.

They say their God is the same as the British, but the British are not the true children of God, because they have the wrong lineage.

In one way, I can see their point. They called themselves Muslims. They despise the pomp and ceremony of the English, and any idea that a king can lead the church. My problem with them is the rigidity in their practices. There is a time each day for all men to pray. They must all point in the right direction. I cannot say that God told me this, but these practices are as ludicrous to me as a king representing God."

"There is a warrior kingdom in the East that calls their ruler a man-god. The ancient Egyptians did that, too." I remembered from my classes.

"Perhaps, you will see enough of the world to study them all for me." he said. "It is like they are all shadows of the spiritual, to me. None of them satisfy me. There is something missing. Some bridge I have not found.

Soon, it will not matter." he said with resolution. "Soon, I will pass over into the spiritual, whether I have found the bridge or not."

"The British talk of some part of their God being a door." I volunteered.

"I guess there could be something to that." he said. "I just can't see being led to the door by a king.

This is exhausting." he said, frustrated. "How far are we from the nest you told me about? We could discuss these matters for years and not know anymore than we do now. That is one of my reasons for not wanting to go into these matters with you."

"Thank you, Master, even if we have not resolved anything." I said.

CHAPTER 22

We proceeded only a short ways further when the Master let out a joyful shout.

"Look!" he squealed. "I didn't realize it was this time of year already." He pulled up the flap of his cloak and began chasing a large brown blur flying just off the ground.

"Be careful Master." I shouted. "You may be stung." I should have known better. He was obviously renewing another old relationship.

Finally, he scooped the cloth up like a net and brought his hands together to capture the prize.

"Look at this." he said. His voice told me that I was going to be impressed with what I saw.

When I looked into his cupped hands, I saw an ugly bug. It was a common brown beetle, so ordinary we did not even have a name for them. "Master," I said, "I know these bugs. They are common around here. I didn't think they could fly, but I've seen them crawling around all the time."

"You are so right." he joined in happily. "They are common. They don't fly, except when it's the time of the year to mate. That's part of the beauty of it. Look here. Do you see this patch of hair?"

My interest was not aroused very much. How could

such an ordinary insect have any great revelations or mysteries to share with us? Nevertheless, I was learning to trust the Master.

It was a plain dull brown bug about half the size of my thumb. The Master was pointing to a small triangular tuft of tiny hairs just behind the head. The peak of the triangle ended where the wing covers joined to form the body shell.

"Master," I confessed, "I see it, but I cannot see any significance to it."

"Neither did I," he agreed, "not for years. They only fly about a month of the year during mating. Then they crawl around until the next mating season."

"What does that have to do with the tuft of hairs?" I wondered.

"Exactly my point." the Master exclaimed. "I learned that during the beginning of the season only the males fly around. They are the ones that have the patches of hair on their backs. The females are almost exactly the same except they don't have hair on their backs. The females begin to fly about two weeks after the males."

"Perhaps, the hair is a means of identification." I suggested.

"That's the same thing I thought in the beginning. I'm still not positive which one is the female. I have only assumed it from the nature of their mating behavior, but there is much more to the mystery. I don't want to tell you. Hopefully, I can show you, if it's not too early. This is the first flyer I've seen this year."

"Whatever do you mean Master. What is too early?"

"You may get to see." he said. "Get your legs ready. I'm going to depend on you to keep up with the bug if he flies too fast for me." With that, he opened his hand.

It took the beetle a few seconds to get his bearings. It took a few more for the clumsy creature to unfold his wing flaps. At last, his wings began to beat. He made a low pitched hum that reminded me of a bumble bee. He was painfully slow and unsteady as he rose to waist high and began his journey, again.

The bug appeared to be drunk as it flew. It veered to the right or left often without any semblance of control. Once that problem appeared stabilized, he managed to fly straight for a short time. Suddenly, he dipped wildly down and nearly crashed into the ground. A flight correction caused the insect to soar back above my head. Almost immediately it dived again nearly as badly as it did the first time.

It was no problem keeping up with such an awkward flyer. Somehow, it was still managing to fly in a generally straight line. Little by little the Master began to fall behind.

"Where are we going, Master?" I called back over my shoulder.

"He's looking for a mate." the Master answered from behind. "Just stay with him. I'll catch up with you."

I could tell by his voice that he was not winded. He simply could not make his ancient limbs move any faster.

The beetle seemed to choose to fly in the sun. He avoided any shade, only to return to his original course after going around it.

We reached a particularly open area. It looked almost like a meadow. The bug rose up and dived toward the ground. Then, it began to hover and circle wildly around a naked stem sticking up from the ground.

From a ways behind me, I heard the Master's voice. "Good, I remember this patch from other years. A few of them are up already."

While I was trying to figure out what he was talking about, the bug landed clumsily on an ugly brown seed pod on the end of the stem.

Soon, it was obvious the beetle was not trying to land. It's wings were flapping in a wild frenzy as it clutched the seed pod.

The insect was trying to fly away with the seed pod, but it could not. The pod seemed firmly attached to the stem. The bug could only manage to lift the pod about a finger's length. Both the pod and the bug flopped over backwards. The beetle struck another part of the plant I'd failed to notice. It was nothing more than a tufted ball located a little higher on the thin stem.

The Master caught up and was standing next to me.

"Isn't it beautiful?" he asked.

"Beautiful?" I replied. "It looks crazy to me."

"Indeed," he agreed, "crazy to reproduce."

"What?" I shot back in disbelief. "Master, why would a bug try to mate with a plant?"

"Perhaps, the bug doesn't see the plant the same way we do. Perhaps the bug sees the plant as a potential mate."

"That is crazy." I said with conviction. "What possible purpose could be served in that? Does the beetle break the seed pod open and spread the seeds?"

"So, you think it is a seed pod, do you? I think it is a flower."

"Master," I said carefully. I did not want to be disrespectful, but I was already pretty well versed in biology. "Flowers are the reproductive organs of plants. They have two parts. The petals serve to help bees and other insects to locate the reproductive parts. Each flower is both male and female. That seed pod is too far away from the tuft to be a part of the flower."

"What if this is not an ordinary flower?" he asked. "What if this particular flower was designed for this particular bug? What if this bug is the only insect that ever has anything to do with this plant? If the pod attracts the beetle to the plant while it is looking for a mate, then the pod serves the purpose of a petal does it not?"

"That is impossible." I declared somewhat indignantly. Now, it was I who was a little offended.

"Oh really." he shot back with a hint of amusement. "Come look at this and explain it to me."

The beetle had given up attacking the seed pod, but it moved only a short distance. It was angrily buzzing as it worked with all its strength to pry another pod from its stem, with the same results. The beetle was flopping and straining to fly away. Each attempt caused it to be flipped over onto another tuft on the end of the stem.

The Master raised the hem of his cloak again. When the bug finally gave up its quest, he caught it easily. Again, he showed me his prize proudly.

"Look here." here he said pointing to the back of our captive. "Do you remember the patch of hair on the back? Look at it now after only two flowers."

I stared in disbelief. The hair was full of an oddly colored dust. It could only be pollen.

"It has to be pollen." I said apologetically.

"That was the only conclusion I could come to." he said with the voice of a scientist.

"But Master," I said in bewilderment. "How can that be possible?"

"For me," he said, "it is possible because God made it for me to find. In seven or eight days, this field will be filled with the flowers. It will also be alive with the sound of hundreds of these beetles. Each will be straining unsuccessfully to mate with the petal. In so doing they will be transferring the pollen from plant to plant.

I have watched this plant and bug for twenty-five

years. It is always the same every year. Not one other insect will pay the least bit of attention to these ugly weeds.

In twelve or fourteen days, you will see twice as many beetles in the air mating. The ugly flowers will get no more attention. When they mate, the beetle on the bottom never has hair. They will be almost exactly the same size and color as the brown lobe on the stem.

Ten to twelve days later all the bugs will be crawling around on their bellies, again. The tiny tufts at the end of the stems will have released their seeds.

They will sprout and grow during the rainy season and next year at this time barren stems will shoot up to entice a new generation of hairy beetles.

"Master," I wondered, "why did you say that God designed them for you to find?"

"You don't think it happened by chance do you?" he laughed. "Did the plants begin to notice the hairy beetles flying around uselessly and start to talk through their roots? 'We should feel sorry for that ugly bug. Let us change our children to attract the bugs with the hair on their backs. That will allow them to have a part with all the rest of the insects that help plants to reproduce.' How would the plants reproduce while they changed their shape to accommodate the size and shape of the beetle?

Can you imagine the beetles joining together in a discussion? 'Have you seen those ugly flowers that rise up just as we begin to feel the urge to mate? They are so ugly the rest of the bugs and bees avoid them. We must arrange to begin growing hair on our backs. Right in the middle. Right above the wing flaps. That should accommodate them nicely. We must also work it out that our own mates are not neglected. Only the males should grow hair. We'll have them come into heat a few days before the females. Once the flowers have been pollinated, we can perform our dance for each other.'"

"Master, please." I interrupted. "Are you trying to make fun of me?"

"No, no of course not." he assured me. "It is as I have told you. God has constructed all that is out here into a beautiful mystery. Things that seem so simple and unimportant are really part of an elaborate cloth stitched with individual threads by God, to make an endless pattern.

He whispers to me that nothing is by chance. He watches every plant and bug. He knows every animal by name, like I know you. That is how awesome He is. He tells me to learn of Him by watching them."

"Master," I said, "that is a beautiful thought. I wish above all that I could hear that voice, too."

"I have done it again, haven't I?" he said reproachfully to himself.

"Boy, listen to me. Do not pay any attention to any of what I have said to you about God, unless you can honestly say that He has spoken to you. When people say that God talks to them, we put them out of town, don't we?"

"Master," I replied, "We put out the people who say that God has talked to them, and then act very strangely."

He began to howl with laughter. He danced and stamped his feeble feet into the ground a few times.

"Well, look at us!" he roared. "We are standing in the wilderness looking at ugly flowers with one petal and bugs with hair on their backs." His eyes glowed with the humor of his joke.

I did not speak, but in my heart I thanked whatever God there was that He had put the Master in my life.

CHAPTER 23

As soon as we began walking again, I noticed that we were almost at the bird's nest.

We approached the nest cautiously, and waited until both parent birds left the nest. The two chicks were just as I'd remembered them. The larger bird was so obviously not like the parent birds, it was hard to believe the parent birds could not tell the impostor was not theirs. It was hard to believe they would feed the chick instead of killing it and feeding it to theirs. The robber bird was so much bigger and stronger, it seemed it could easily kill the cowchaser and have the nest all to itself.

"Let's go on." he suggested. "It is early in the season for cowchaser hatching. Perhaps we can find another nest with younger chicks. I know of several other trees that have had cowchaser nests in other years. If we can find one, I think you will enjoy what you see."

It did not take long. The Master led me directly to another nest. It had a robber bird in it and a cowchaser egg. "Excellent," the Master exclaimed, "we will be able to find what we're looking for." He turned and led me on.

The next nest had two chicks in it. The cowchaser

chick was only hours old. It was just as the Master described. The robber bird chick was vigorous and healthy. The newborn cowchaser was little more than a lump of flesh. Its hairless head was barely able to point itself weakly towards us hoping for food from any source appearing above it.

"The robber bird is only a couple of days older than the cowchaser," whispered the Master, "but just look at it." The robber bird was vigorous and healthy. It was already very capable of bounding across the nest and placed itself squarely before us, eyeball to eyeball, to demand food from us. By comparison the cowchaser chick was pathetically weak and helpless. Its head wobbled precariously hoping for some tidbit, but soon it collapsed into the hairless mound of flesh.

Once the robber bird was convinced that we did not bring any food, it turned its attention back to a fly buzzing about the nest. Each time the fly landed on its stepsibling, the robber bird lunged at it wildly.

"It has not refined its movements enough to catch the fly, yet." observed the Master. "but perhaps its efforts are enough to explain the mystery to you."

"Do you mean that the robber bird is actually protecting the young cowbird?" I asked, not quite believing the simplicity of the assumption. It was unthinkable to me that the solution could be so practical.

"It has always seemed very logical to me." he said. "Look at how irritating we find the biting, sucking flies. They would be able to chew the helpless chick to death if there were enough of them. It must be something like that. I told you, I never saw a cowchaser chick survive from a nest that did not have a robber bird in it."

"That means there is a good reason why the cowchaser parents feed and care for the robber bird." I said.

"And it would mean that the robber birds are not lazy thieving horrible parents, who leave the rearing of their children to other good birds." the Master added.

At that moment the robber bird chick actually caught the marauding fly and gulped it down gleefully.

"Yes! Yes!" exalted the Master.

This time as the Master began dancing his dance, I felt like joining him.

"There is always a reason." he sang." You built purpose into everything."

He stopped singing and turned to me.

"It seems to me that we must have a god for every whim of life and nature. It is the way man is. We have to make up gods for things we can't understand. We have whimsical and mischievous gods to explain what seems to be mischievous acts in nature. My conclusion is that if we cannot see Him in any situation, it is only because our seeing is limited.

One of the parent birds returned and chased us away with a fluttering attack. Once we were safely driven off, it dutifully returned to the nest with a beetle clutched in its mouth.

We stayed at the nest for several parental encounters watching in between feedings. We watched the Robber bird catch two more flies with increasing flare.

"It is almost as though the robber bird was fly fishing, using the cowchaser chick for bait." ventured the Master. "Its parents put it there so that it could catch the flies trying to eat the bait, and in so doing they provided a service to the parent birds. How wonderful it all is."

He put his arm around my neck and pulled me purposely to himself. As we stood in the path, he held me for a long moment. I perceived that there were many things being said in that embrace. One of them was "Good-bye."

"You are a fine boy." he said finally. "Your grandfather would be so proud of you."

My head was against his shoulder and I could hear his words two ways. His embrace was like salve to my soul. It covered a wound I did not know was there until treated with the medicine of that embrace.

I did not speak until he released me. I wanted to savor the moment as long as it would last. Finally, he pushed me to arms length.

"Master," I confessed, "If I have been my grandfather for you, then you, also, have been my grandfather for me. I felt as though your embrace was his."

His eyes gleamed at me with approval. We both meant so much to each other, and yet, we were unified by a man I'd never met.

"The day has escaped us." he said looking around. "We better start moving or we will be on the road after the sun goes down."

Although he could not walk very quickly, the Master maintained a steady pace and still managed to carry on a lively conversation. As soon as we entered through the city gates, he sent me on home. He ask that I bring the microscope back the next day. He would like to look at water from the river. He had heard that water was filled with tiny invisible bugs.

CHAPTER 24

My feet flew down the streets home. Father's return was in the back of my mind all day, but it was covered up by all the things a conversation with the Master led to. I had nothing planned. I could only hope Father had not returned.

Faude met me about a block from home. He had already been to the Master's hut. I could tell that he was greatly relieved to see me and I knew immediately what he would tell me.

"Your father arrived early this afternoon." he said. "He has been most concerned about you. I told him you have been coming home quite late, but it still concerned him.

He is waiting for you at dinner. I suggest you go directly to him."

I tried to hurry like a man would. I did not run with arms and legs flailing about, like a child rushing into his father's arms. I wanted to look purposeful, but as soon as I saw him, hope rose within me, and I rushed to him. He had been a boy once. He walked the road alone.

"Father, I want to thank you." I gushed. "In the beginning, I did not have any idea why you were sending me to the Master.

The Master told me so much about Grandfather. I wish I could have known him. At first, I thought you intended me to teach him. Isn't that incredible?"

I laughed at the ridiculousness of the thought, hoping father would join me, but he remained sitting impassively.

"He said he became your teacher when you were four or five. What an experience that must have been."

I was out of control. Words flew from my mouth and scattered like sown seeds in a wind.

"I lectured him on economics and geometry the first day. Can you imagine me lecturing him?

The first time he danced, I did not know what to do. I could never have imagined an old man acting like that."

I could not detect any change in Father's bearing. I wondered whether the Master danced when he had Father for a student. I kept looking for some change, some softening in him as a childhood remembrance warmed his heart. I knew it would happen if I could find the right words. I tried to cover him with my recent experiences with the Master. hoping that one would do the trick.

One after another, the story sentences flew out of me.

"He took me out on the Flood Road!" I exclaimed. "Can you imagine what that was like for a city boy like me?" Each time I asked a question, I paused slightly. As soon as I saw there would be no response, another thought flew out of my mouth.

"He showed me things I never saw in the books.

We studied ants. They are farmers, like men, except they farm tiny white aphids. I helped him discover that fact with the microscope you brought me from

Delhi.

One day we almost walked over a cobra. The Master saw it first.

Another day, I'm sure I heard a rodent running from me get eaten by a cobra or some other large snake.

I learned that robber birds lay their eggs in cowchaser nests. The robber bird chick helps protect the cowchaser chick from flies."

Father remained attentive, but unresponsive. I assumed that could only mean one thing. He was waiting for me to tell him of my grand journey down the road.

"All of that pales," I said, pausing to build suspense, "to the lessons I learned when I walked the road alone.

I could not make it the first day," I confessed, "but I did the second.

I was still scared to death. I didn't see a thing." I laughed. Surely, this would bring something out of him, and it did. He leaned forward.

"Are you saying that he sent you across the Flood Road alone?" he asked. He did not show any visible emotion.

"Yes, and it was wonderful." I rushed to say more. "The Master said you walked a road alone, too, but not that road. He would not tell me whether you were successful or not, the first time. The Master said it was a different time and place, so it didn't matter."

This time I waited for Father to respond.

His expression never changed. He rose from the table and walked to a window. "That is correct," he said coldly. He turned to me, and said, "The old fool sent me down a road I walked a thousand times. I knew every stupid tree, and bush, and bird's nest by heart." His disbelief and anger grew more obvious with each word.

"He was trying to kill you to pay me back for giving you the best education possible."

"Father, I'm sure you are mistaken." I assured him. "He spoke of you and Grandfather in the most loving terms. He talked often of how much he loved Grandfather and how much he owed to him.

Only today, he said that he was ready to die, now. He felt that God had given him his last request, to see me and pay his debt to Grandfather."

"So, the old idiot is still tearing himself apart with that one god foolishness. Did he try to fill your mind with that nonsense, too?" he demanded.

"We talked of it," I said defensively, "but I had to force him. He did not want to speak of it. He said it was like a blessing and a curse, and he didn't want to be responsible for me."

"It was only because he did not have time to indoctrinate you." Father said bitterly. "His lessons always left that to be our conclusion. Did we see the pattern? Did we see the structure?

He knew all the time where he was trying to lead us."

Finally, Father drew up close to me. He put both hands on the table and moved in very close to me. "Did he really send you down the road, alone?" he asked. His tone told me something was very wrong. His question gave me one final opportunity find the words to heal the moment.

"Yes Father, but it was a wonderful experience. It has changed . ."

"Enough!" he roared. "Let us go see this MASTER!" he emphasized the word sarcastically. "We will inform him that you have completed your lessons with him while you still have blood in your veins."

He was out the door before I had a chance to intervene further. I was completely bewildered. How could things have worked out like this? This was supposed to have been a grand homecoming. My father was supposed to see that he had a new, different, more capable son. Chaos seemed to reign supreme. Instead of gaining a grandfather, I was going to lose the second most important person in my life. The same emptiness that invaded my body when my mother died returned.

How could life be such a cruel mess?

CHAPTER 25

"Faude!" Father called. "We are going to see Teacher." I recognized the nickname Grandfather gave the Master. The way Father said it the word was filled with contempt.

He did not wait for me. He was in the street by the time I caught up with him. Our conversation was over. I tried to intervene. I had to run to keep up with him. I would get four or five steps ahead and make my plea. I said that I used the wrong words. I told him the Master's lessons changed the way I would live the rest of my life. He would not answer. He passed by me without breaking stride. Then I would have a few moments to gather my next argument as I ran to get ahead of him again.

"The lessons helped me, too." he admitted finally and slowed to a stop. "I was not sent into the wild until I learned the lessons of the wild. The old fool almost killed my only son." he said passionately. "Who will I give my business to if you die? Your mother carried my heart with her to the grave. I cannot give myself to another woman. I have no more desire." His face was helpless, stretched in tearless anguish.

He began walking at a driven pace again. Nothing I did or said had any effect. It was only after we passed to the poor side of town, that he slowed once more. We began to speak in low hushed whispers.

"Father," I said, "you said that mother carried your heart into the grave. She did that to me also. We are both the same. Mother's death joined us both in the same sorrow.

The Master joined me together with my grandfather. He has helped me heal my sorrow a little."

"My father was a wonderful man." father admitted, losing some of his emotion and urgency.

"Now we also have the Master in common." I reasoned. "It will be good for both of us. Besides, it was good for me to learn of my grandfather."

"It was his folly, too." my father snorted. Somehow my words caused his anger to flame again. His pace picked up and regained its urgency. "It was the railroad that prospered your grandfather, not Teacher. Your grandfather never would have become any more than a merchant if the railroad left for the highlands from a different city. He never understood that."

"The Master said Grandfather told him that he had trained many people who could do his job. That was why Grandfather was able to let the Master teach you." I argued, defending both of them.

"That may be true," countered my father, "but all those tasks demanded completion. Father would have found the people to do the work. It was the railroad that changed your grandfather's fortunes, not Teacher."

We found the Master sitting with the company of his neighbors. He rose excitedly when he saw Father walking up. The Master came forward to greet my father. He tried to hug him, but Father held him away.

"Teacher, I must speak to you privately." he said coldly.

"Of course," the Master answered and led the way to his hut.

"You have a wonderful son." the Master began. "He is the image of his grandfather."

"Is that why you tried to kill him?" Father asked sarcastically. The anger in him began to boil and pour out of him.

"Is that why you put him out on the road alone, to die." his voice became hysterical. "Has your displeasure with me caused you to gain revenge through his death?"

The Master did not flinch.

"He is a beautiful child." he countered. "I have learned so much from him. The world is so amazing today. They keep inventing new things that old men like me can't understand."

"Don't try to play with me!" my father shouted. "I will not stand for it. Do not try to treat me as one of your children."

"I do not understand you." the Master said. There was a hint of coldness in his voice. "Perhaps you will explain yourself to me." It was a polite request, but it carried with it an authority that hinted at their former relationship.

"You sent my son . . . my only son onto a wild road, alone." Father said carefully restraining his anger until he inhaled. Then his composure burst. "He was not prepared. He could have been killed on the road and you would have been his killer as surely as if you did it with a knife."

The Master looked at him intently, but he did not back away.

"He could have been killed, you say. I sent you down the road, too. You could have been killed, too."

"It was not the same, and you know it!" my father roared. "You prepared me for years before you sent me out alone. You are trying to torment me. You are trying to get back at me for not sending the boy to you long ago."

"Is that what you think?" the Master asked sadly. "I was your teacher for years. You know me well. At least you knew me well, before you became such an important man on the river."

My father lowered his head. "I cannot think of any other reason, Teacher. What were your trying to do?" Father retorted. His anger and suspicion retreated with each word.

"What did you send him to me to learn?" the Master asked. His voice was still soft, but I could tell that he expected Father to answer. I was not used to watching my father answer questions.

"What does that have to do with anything?" Father shot back angrily.

"I presumed when you sent Faude to talk to me you wanted me to attempt to teach him the lessons of life. He already knows how to read and count far better than I. I determined that in a few minutes on the first day. What else was I to conclude?"

My father erupted. "He could have been killed! You old fool. Can't you see that?" Father was not used to people challenging him.

"What did you want me to teach him?" the Master repeated patiently.

"I wanted you to teach him, but I did not intend for you to endanger him." Father explained.

"No. . No." insisted the Master saying the word distinctly, "What did you want me to teach him? You are upset with how I taught him. I want you to tell me what you expected me to teach him."

Father was quiet. The Master waited staring at him intently.

"I do not know how to answer your question." Father conceded, finally.

"It is a simple question." the Master replied. "You could have sent him to me when he was four or five. I could have taught him to read and count then. It would have been the most obvious thing to do, but you waited. He will be thirteen next week. You are sending him down river to Calcutta. You must have had a reason for sending him to me now." He was insistent. It was clear that the Master was not going to let the issue die without an answer.

"I had to keep my promise to my father. He made me promise to send my sons to you. I got so busy, I neglected my duty. When I finally decided to send him to Calcutta, I realized I never kept my promise. Naturally, I undertook it at once." Father's composure returned as he spoke. He cupped his hands together when he used the word promise to indicate closure. It was all a little theatrical and I could tell he was trying to placate the Master.

"Shame! Shame on you!" the Master cried. He pointed his finger at him accusingly. "I said you knew me, but I know you, too. How dare you try to lie to me, like that."

Father lowered his head again.

"I am not trying to be harsh with you." the Master spoke reassuringly. "I have a purpose in this. What did you want me to teach the boy?"

"He is going to Calcutta," Father began in a halting voice, "I wanted you to prepare him . . ." He stopped speaking again. "I know . . . I know that he has done very well in school, but I have been able to watch over him . . . ."

"But in Calcutta," the Master fed him the words.

"In Calcutta my name is one of hundreds, even thousands. My name cannot watch over him there."

It was a unique moment for me. I knew my father as a very important man. When he spoke other men stopped to listen. I could not imagine a place with so many important men that they made him ordinary.

"What happens to the boy will not matter to anyone but me." he wailed. "His mother is dead. I have only one son. . ." his voice trailed away.

"And so, you wanted me to teach him not to die." The Master finished the thought for him.

"No, that is not what I wanted you to teach him." Father was annoyed again. His intensity began to rise.

"Then what?" the Master insisted innocently.

Father did not move. He stared intently at the floor.

"He is a good boy," he began in a halting voice, "but there is so much he does not know about people, about life. Teacher, I know I was angry with you. I have the deepest respect for you and your instruction. I honestly did not realize that I never sent the boy to you, until I decided to send him to Calcutta. After his mother died . ." his voice trailed away again.

The Master did not rescue him. He waited for Father to finish. "Yes, all right." Father said weakly. "I did not want him to die. I want him to live and have many sons. That is why I became so enraged at you. You were supposed to understand my fears."

"I suppose that I did," confided the Master, "but how was I supposed to teach it to the boy without exposing him to danger? When we talked of death, we spoke much of death's uncertainties. A cough today can mean death is a day or two away. You know that these things are true and unavoidable."

"I know," Father agonized, "but to expose him to the dangers of the wilds. He knows nothing about them, how will that ensure anything?"

"My friend, . . my student," the Master said compassionately, "you know that nothing can be assured."

"He is my only son!" my father cried. "After his mother died, I buried myself in the business. She was different from other women. There was a deepness in her that took me in. When she left me, she took a part of me in her ashes with her. She left a part of herself with me in the boy. There are times I cannot bear to look at him." His voice shook with the emotion, and then there were tears. A few of them streamed down his face, before he wiped them away.

"I love him more than I love my life," Father wailed. "I cannot tell him, or I will never stop crying for her."

I wanted to run to him, but something held me back. Part of me was warmed and reassured, finally, that my father loved me. Another part felt as though I was eavesdropping on another student's lesson. I stayed back in the shadows on the far side of the room.

"Perhaps, the question should be asked." the Master continued. "What did I teach you? What did you remember that you wished me to impart to the boy?"

Regaining his composure, he recollected the memories of his youth, then he lifted his eyes.

"You taught me everything, Teacher."

"I taught you to read and count." the Master corrected him. "By the time you were his age," he motioned to me, "you were unloading steamships.

You used to work like a dog." he laughed. "Your father was so proud of you. Do you remember?"

Father agreed without emotion. It was as though he considered the conversation pointless.

"You worked so hard at everything you did, even then." the Master remembered for him.

"I wanted him to recognize me." father said as though somehow that recognition was still lacking somehow.

"You know that he did." insisted the Master. "He was amazed at you. You learned everything so quickly. How he loved to work with you. He told me, that he had to order you to stop working and eat, or to come to see me.

Remember all the times your father came to walk and talk with me, and you chose not to come?"

"It seemed so pointless to me." Father said. "A sunset comes every night. You can only talk about one thing for so long, then talk becomes meaningless. When you work, you can see what you've accomplished. You and father could talk for hours, day after day. You would go on endlessly from one subject to another. I know that Father was not happy with me, but I could not abide the waste of time. Father could not understand. I know that I let him down."

"On the contrary," the Master objected, "your father and I often discussed what a great businessman you would become. His concerns for you were in another area, entirely."

The Master paused. It was not his way to go into a subject uninvited.

"What could that possibly be, Teacher?" he asked. "Everything spins off a man's work."

"He was concerned about what kind of husband and father you would be." the Master answered politely.

"I gave my wife and child everything I had." Father replied without any hint of guilt or anger. "I did not realize what a hold she had on me until she was gone. I would give all I have accumulated and begin again, if I could have her back one more day. I would look into her eyes for the day. I would gaze upon the pureness in her soul, and fill myself with the beauty of it."

The Master raised his hand to stop Father. "Look at

your son." he ordered softly.

Father's composure crumbled.

"I cannot!" he sobbed.

"You must!" insisted the Master. "Look at the purity of his soul, the beauty of his heart. You just said you would give everything you have to see her again, for a day. If you look, you will see her in the boy."

"Please, stop this." Father whispered weakly, "You are torturing me with your words."

"There is a purpose." the Master reassured him. "You must see something, I see. You must let me be your teacher one more time."

"I do not know what you're getting at Teacher." He was not the same man I knew as my father. His whole bearing was weak and vulnerable. I'd never seen him like that in my life, even when Mother died.

"It is the boy." the Master said simply. "You must recognize why you sent him to me. Then you will understand why I sent him down the Flood Road. I had to do it, because you did not do your job. You knew that he was not ready to go to a distant city, which, if you think about it is a different kind of wilderness. The dangers there will come from the people he meets and follows. The boy was not educated in these areas and you remembered me."

My father's head hung very low.

"I think I can see what you're saying." he said in a solemn voice.

"Once I saw how advanced he was in reading and counting, I knew you could only have one reason for sending him to me. You wanted me to prepare him for the unknown uncertainties waiting for him in Calcutta, and the rest of his life for that matter.

Is my hypothesis correct?" he asked with the assurance that it was.

The Master turned and stole a sly moment with my eye. He used the word I taught him.

"Yes, I suppose you could say it that way." Father replied with a broken weariness. He looked as though he had lost his identity. I wasn't sure he really did agree with the Master. It was clear, he was in no mood to dispute anything.

"You did not give me any time." the Master continued without complaining. "Once I saw he was a good boy, who was not given to rebellion or disrespect, I had only one place left to go. Unfortunately, life has little meaning unless it is fenced in by death. It is so difficult for young people to understand that. You may be upset with me, but I felt I had to let him confront the possibility of imminent death to acquaint him with fear.

He will never again know fear as a stranger. He learned so much. He has so much to teach you.

You must begin immediately to defeat your fear."

The Master moved close to Father and firmly stuck his finger in his chest.

"You must not run away anymore, hiding yourself in your work. If you do not give yourself immediately to him, you will surely lose him in Calcutta. Even if he does not die, you will lose his heart."

It appeared that my father was going to try to mount some kind of protest, but the Master cut him off. "You said you would give up everything to have your wife for one more day. Be courageous and give up everything for one week. Be with your son. Go to Calcutta with him. Do not send Faude with him. Take him yourself. Go with him tomorrow into the tall grasses. Talk and discover things with him."

"But, I have obligations." Father sputtered.

"Indeed you do!" exclaimed the Master as he sprang into some new sort of a dance, "and your obligation is to him." He ended emphatically with his hands upon my shoulders. I kept my eyes to the floor. I was afraid to hope. I was sure Father would say, 'My word is my bond. I must make my appointments.' I did not hear a sound from him, but I was afraid to look.

"You must do this, and you must do it now." the Master insisted softly. "You may not get another chance."

"I do not think I know how." my father pleaded.

"The boy will teach you." the Master assured him confidently. "It will only be a new road for you. He has been down it many times, since his mother died. He will make it easy for you."

The Master began to push me toward him. He did not say a word until we were next to each other.

"Hold your son," he ordered. "He needs you and you need him. You do not need to say words. Let your grief and fear pass through your body to him, and his to you. You will find that his fears are a salve for your grief, and your fears will make him strong and resolute in his determination to return to you."

He pushed us together, and then immediately out the door. We did not talk much on the way home. I fell asleep as soon as I laid down, too mentally exhausted to think about what was happening to me.

CHAPTER 26

The blast from one of the steamships woke me in the morning. It was departing. I was sure Father was on it. A helpless emptiness filled me. I leaped out of bed and ran through the bedroom door.

Father was sitting in a chair in the dining area. He motioned for me to come to him.

"I sent Faude downriver to cancel my meetings for this week." He began. "I do not know how to follow Teacher's instructions, but I know that I must."

We spent that week together. It was not all easy. We saw different things in different ways. Father told me many times how much I was like my grandfather. He went with me to Calcutta. Whenever he came downriver, he never failed to schedule at least one day just to see me.

I received word two weeks after I started school that the Master died in his sleep. I did not know whether to be sad or happy. He profoundly affected my life. I purposed to try to live my life in a way that allowed me to reach old age with the same fullness I saw in him.

Through the years my classes on the Flood Road, my lessons in the tall grasses, came to my aid many times. They would prove to be the center of my decision making processes. Sometimes, I decided to run. Other times I had to stand my ground in the face of incredible odds. There were times the power of fear shook me to the roots of my being, before I finally recognized my old visitor and identified him for who he was.

My father became great and traveled all of India. What he left me enabled me to do business and travel all over the world.

I remembered the Master in all my travels. I remembered and searched out more information concerning this one great god that he could not name. It was as much a search for truth on my behalf, but it seemed that my observations and conclusions always led me to agree with the Master's.

Finally, my understanding was fulfilled on a stormy night in England. I was conversing with a priest of the King of England. He informed me of the error within the Master's information. He informed me that there was indeed a name. It was the name of a King, but not the King of England. His God was a king who laid down his nobility to be low born among men. He became a farmer, a shepherd actually, and cared for all of the sheep of God. The sheep were not animals but people. The Father had given His Son to be a shepherd and a king over mankind, a ruler and a servant at once. In that service, it became necessary that He die to protect and secure His flock. In that death, He made it possible for all who were his sheep to enter His nobility and to be called a child of God.

I could not understand these things, still I could not end our conversation. So much of what the priest said plugged into my memories of the Master. At times, I even considered that the priest might be a spy planted by some unknown enemy to influence me and gain some business advantage. Too many of the things he said were almost as if they had come from the master's mouth. I had told the story of my lesson's in the tall grasses many times over the years. Someone had to have coached him.

I became upset several times. It was all so improbable. Each time I threw up an argument, the priest answered it with an example that carried me back to my walks with the Master.

"Why would a king have to die for his people?"

The priest smiled and said, "There is a great gap that stands between man and God. It is evil. Man, alone in all creation, is separated from God by evil."

It was the Master's conclusion!

"Nature," he said, "cannot be separated from God. It is an awesome painting, painted by God to reveal who He is and how He works."

It was the Master, again.

"Have you noticed in your travels how many religions rely upon a sacrifice of blood to become right with their gods?" he asked. "It was the Son sent from the Father, to be the king and servant. The king lived as a servant and died as a sacrifice to make a bridge to the Father, to reach across the gap."

"The Master looked for a bridge." I told him. "He knew it must be there somewhere."

I became upset when he brought a son of god into the story. The Master had been adamant, there was One God.

The priest laughed and said there was even another, a Spirit, who remained and moved about on the earth to bring men like me and the Master to know the son, and through Him pass over the bridge to the Father. "It was the Spirit," he said, who had prepared me, by the occurrences in my life for this night. It was the Spirit that brought his words alive in my heart.

By that time, I was ready to leave. How could one God break himself into three pieces and still be one? It was ridiculous. I could not imagine such a thing. I was too old and I still did not like being made the fool.

That was when it happened.

The priest began to laugh innocently. It was the Master's laugh. I could hardly contain myself. I felt as though I was a boy again. "So you are convinced, that this is an impossibility?" he asked in a leading sort of a voice. I heard a distant warning from my childhood. I was back in the Master's hut. I was being led like a child again, by one who knew more than I did. Still, I had to hold my ground.

"It is almost preposterous." I said. "You are playing with me like a child."

"You did tell me that the Master told you to remember that fact for the rest of your life."

"Yes, yes, of course." I agreed. Irritation was beginning to replace patience.

"Both I and the Master have identified the world around us as a canvas used by God to reveal himself. Isn't that so?"

"Yes, it was what has intrigued me about our conversation. So much of what you have said was central in the Master's teaching. It seems impossible that it could be a coincidence. That does not mean that I can begin to accept the idea that some strange part of God has broken itself off from the main part to bring me to the point to where I will believe that one God can have three parts. Even the Master would have demanded a very obvious proof of such a profound impossibility."

"You tell me then," the priest asked softly. His eyes twinkled as they gazed into my soul. "Which is the egg? Is it the shell? Can it only be the yellow? What is an egg?"

I was dumbfounded as I searched for some answer that would uphold my reasoning. The foolishness of a child flowed over me and took away my false sense of pride.

"I do not know what to say." I said weakly. "I didn't think this was possible."

"The egg is a brushstroke of God." he said for me. "It is three things at once and it is the beginning of life."

That night I began a new journey of discovery. I crossed a bridge that led me to a God I could call Father. I received a king who served me even to death, and I began to follow a Spirit who led me and showed Himself to me in my life, day by day. My life became filled with wonderful questions, whose answers gave me new questions to ask.

I think the Master would have approved.

It was on that day I became truly rich. I find my old age to be full and complete. To this day, I am thankful. I know now, that the Master did not curse me, rather he blessed me, and I have been blessed.

I have even lived long enough to tell my story to you.

About the Author

Stan Hahn currently is an adult education teacher for the Orange County Public School System in Orlando, Florida. For the past ten years, he has taught a variety of adult classes from employability to juvenile education. Stan is a graduate of Central Michigan University with a BS degree in History and Speech. Stan's extensive background includes work in construction, warehousing, and food services. He has been an active member of The Heart of Florida Civitan, the Florida Literacy Coalition, the A.C.E. (Adult and Community Educators) of Florida, the C.T.A. (Certified Teachers Association) and the Teamsters. He and his wife, Nellwyn, are raising two children, Heather and Jason, in Lake Mary, Florida.